LOUDER THAN WORDS

LOUDER THAN WORDS

Ten Employee Engagement Steps that Drive Results

BOB KELLEHER

BLKB
PUBLISHING

To my lifelong best friend and wife Candy,
and the world's best kids: Marissa, Brendan, and Connor.
You mean everything to me.

LOUDER THAN WORDS
Ten Employee Engagement Steps that Drive Results by Bob Kelleher

BLKB Publishing
7336 SE Tibbetts Street
Portland, Oregon, 97206

Unattributed quotations are by Bob Kelleher.

ISBN 978-0-9845329-0-2

Printed in the United States of America

CONTENTS

ABOUT THE AUTHOR

Bob Kelleher is the founder and CEO of The Employee Engagement Group (www.EmployeeEngagment.com), a division of The Kelleher Consulting Group, Inc. and is a noted speaker, thought leader, and consultant who has presented to many respected global companies on the subjects of employee engagement, workforce trends, and leadership. Having been an internal practitioner for many years, his practical approach, willingness to share best practices, and enthusiastic and passionate delivery have proven to be a winning formula for audiences throughout the world.

Before opening his own consulting business, Bob was the Chief Human Capital Officer for AECOM, a Fortune 500 global professional services firm with 45,000 employees located in 450 offices throughout the world. Before joining AECOM in 2005, Bob was Executive Vice President of Organizational Development and Chief Operating Officer for ENSR, a Massachusetts-based, 2,300-employee international environmental consulting firm (now part of AECOM), where he spearheaded award-winning employee engagement programs and initiatives.

Bob actively participates in various industry roundtables and associations, and is often the keynote speaker at conferences and annual strategic planning meetings for organizations such as The Conference Board, Linkage, Human Capital Institute, the Northeast Human Resources Association (NEHRA), Aberdeen Group, Communitelligence, and Melcrum. He is the recipient of numerous awards, including the prestigious NEHRA's 2008 John Erdlen "5 Star" Award (2008); a 2008 AECOM Excellence Award; ENSR's 2007 President's Award; and the Wingate Partners' 2006 Beasely Leadership Award.

Bob holds a BS in Education and an MBA, and resides in Danvers MA with his wife and three children.

ACKNOWLEDGEMENTS

When I left corporate America this past year, I now realize, I was naïve about the time commitment, research, and competing priorities one faces when writing a book: especially when simultaneously launching a successful speaking and consulting business, The Employee Engagement Group (www. EmployeeEngagement.com). Needless to say, this has been one busy year: one in which I have learned a lot about myself (and about the publishing industry). I joke with friends that my next book will be about writing a book!

As someone one who has enjoyed the benefits of a corporate career, I've had to adjust to the realities of being a small entrepreneur – including how to do without the daily friendship and support of my former colleagues. For those of you still on the corporate payroll, I encourage you to hug your IT staff, show appreciation to those who empty your daily bin, and remember to say "thank you" for the little things. Barbara Arruda, my former administrative assistant and lifelong friend: I miss you every day! You are the best!

I am not blessed with the introverted personality of many authors. However, when one partners with terrific people, miracles can occur. There are a multitude of people to thank. Early in my process, I was introduced to my editor and book designer, Liz Batchelder, who over the past year has also become my writing mentor, scheduler, sounding board, supporter, and friend. Thank you to my extended HR, OD, Communications, and IT teams at ENSR, and also at AECOM. When you surround yourself with great and talented people, you can't help but enjoy success. I also want to thank my former leadership team at ENSR, for helping me elevate employee engagement to a key strategic initiative. Because of you, engagement became the foundation of a best in class culture. A special thank you to Bob Weber and Paul Fennelly, ENSR's former board of directors including Chairman Mike Decker, and board member and mentor, Harvard Business School's Ben Shapiro. Engagement starts at the top, and you set a great example during my ENSR years. Thank you Mike Beck for reminding all of us of the importance of perspective.

Also, thank you to AECOM's leadership for embracing engagement, and entrusting me to lead AECOM's employee engagement efforts.

I also want to thank the many colleagues who supported me during the past year, most notably Bob Eubank, Bob Gatti, Clark Willmott, Ryan Kelleher, Chuck Mollor, and Wayne Cascio. The people who helped to polish this book are too many to list, and all of their contributions are much appreciated

– but I would be remiss not to mention the "above and beyond" editorial review and enhancement provided by Jen McKay, Sarah Mann, and Deb Hicks. I should also thank my clients, all of whom shared their time and insight over the past year. This book is made richer by the inclusion of best practices of the Beth Israel Deaconess Medical Center of Boston, The Timberland Company, Cisco Systems, The Beryl Corporation, and Aberdeen Group. Thank you to all for your willingness to share your best practices.

In lieu of having a chance to thank the world's best mom and dad (who are up there watching and smiling on us all), I want to thank my siblings Hugh, Pam, and John, and my late brother Stephen, for helping influence who I am today. Thank you Ed Johnson, my father in law and constant supporter, for always believing in me. To my golf buddies, Ed Burns, John Loughlin, and John Jackson, thanks for keeping me grounded!

And to the world's best kids: you make me proud every single day. When keynoting, I often mention how thankful I am that I get to live in a Gen Y laboratory: studying, watching, and admiring your fascinating generation. Marissa, thank you for bringing me culture and the arts. Brendan and Connor, for your never-ending playfulness (and for occasionally letting me beat you at basketball).

This book is dedicated to my wife Candy. Thank you for being my soul mate, best friend, and number one supporter. Winston Churchill must have had you in mind when he said, "We make a living by what we get; we make a life by what we give." There is no one on the planet who gives more: to me, to our kids, to your students, and to your family and friends. Thank you for being you. Every day.

The measure of success is not whether you have a tough problem to deal with, but whether it is the same problem you had last year.

– JOHN FOSTER DULLES
Former US Secretary of State

INTRODUCTION
THERE'S NO MARKET FOR LIP SERVICE

We've finally reached consensus in the business world: employee engagement is good for the bottom line. In any enterprise you can imagine, at any scale, if you can't satisfy the demands of your clients, you are going to lose business. And the way to reach extraordinary levels of client and customer service is through engaged employees. A company's employees truly are its greatest asset.

But employees are tired of simply hearing that. It's become a cliché. If corporate culture isn't speaking louder than words – if employee engagement is just another program with vague results and halfhearted support – if there is no ACTION and no CHANGE...everyone knows it, and soon productivity will suffer and employees will become cynical.

You may know it already. You may suspect it – something's not quite right at work. In many circles, people talk about leaving as soon as they have the opportunity. They've stopped speaking well of the company to each other – and to potential recruits. There's a prevailing attitude that people are just getting through the day or the week or the month, that they're only there for the paycheck. And there's a growing sense among employees that they've become easily-replaceable commodities (or, worse, that their positions could simply be eliminated to "save payroll"). Whether or not you're in a management position, you can sense that this is just not optimal. Something is out of balance.

There is no quick and easy solution, and just talking about it – even eloquently, even persuasively, even avoiding those tired old management clichés – doesn't accomplish a thing.

What's the Deal?

The good news is that engagement benefits everyone – including management. The reason is that it results in widespread boosts of *discretionary effort*. You may be encountering this term for the first time if you don't follow business jargon closely. Or, you may be an executive who feels he or she is already capturing discretionary effort – or who isn't, but is tired of hearing about it!

If you fall into the latter categories, please bear with a brief and loose explanation: *discretionary effort* is an employee's giving his or her all to any task or activity, as opposed to the *ordinary effort* required to simply get the job done without attracting negative attention. And it's the by-product of an engaged culture.

A popular definition of employee engagement is "the capture of discretionary effort." There are people – including some executives and middle managers – who would admit that they don't always put in their maximum effort every day. They may really apply themselves for that one intriguing assignment or project, but often they're putting in just enough energy to get through the day, and hoping not to feel depleted or deprived by the end of it. Sometimes, maybe frequently, they're erring on the side of conserving energy for themselves, and they're certainly not going to ramp up that energy expenditure without asking, *"What's in it for me?"*

Many definitions of Employee Engagement have resonance. At ENSR, a global consulting firm I worked for that I will reference throughout this book, the definition was "Unlocking Employees' Potential to Drive High Performance." Every organization needs to find a definition that works for their culture, their business, and their employees. But a key theme is the idea of mutual commitment by employer and employee. Examples include:

- Continuously reinforcing "One Team – One Goal."

- Supporting employees who go the extra mile in loyalty and ambassadorship.

- Engaging employees who get their hearts and minds into the business.

- Fostering intellectual understanding and emotional commitment.

- Maintaining an environment where employees think and act as ambassadors for the organization's business goals.

How Do I Know?

I've had a front row seat, with an up-close view of all aspects of how an organization functions (or malfunctions). I'm not an academic or a lifelong consultant. I'm one of the few Human Resource professionals who has not only had a seat at the table – as COO of a 2,000-person professional services firm and then as Chief Human Capital Officer of a 45,000-person firm, I've been at the *head* of the table. With that perspective, I want to share what may be the most important insights of my career to date: *employee engagement is the foundation of a healthy business*. And, shockingly: a *business's customers and clients are not its #1 priority*. Its *employees* have to be. I've heard gasps and observed loaded glances exchanged across boardrooms when I've made this assertion – after all, it's customers and clients who pay the bills, and no one doubts the importance of maintaining their satisfaction and enticing them to employ you further.

But I'll say it once again: *employees are a firm's #1 asset*.

Successful companies know that employees are #1. Certainly clients and customers are "1b," so to speak. But enlightened organizations know that their employees drive client satisfaction, and that without engaged and motivated employees as "1a," you will never achieve truly exemplary client and customer satisfaction.

You might be surprised to hear that clients, after hearing me make a statement that seems to relegate them to a back seat, have often approached me after the meeting or presentation and told me, "I wish this was how our management team felt about us!" After all, clients and customers usually work for companies, too. They want to know that their people aren't just watching the minutes tick by until it's time to clock out. The assurance that the same team will be with you throughout the life of a project, collaboration, or even a simple transaction is worth more than any limp guarantee of commitment a company can make.

Employees' dedication speaks volumes to clients and customers. And to earn and benefit from that dedication, every business needs to be constantly, continuously speaking *louder than words* to its people.

It's Not a "People" Issue. It's a Profitability Issue

The late management guru Peter Drucker said it best when he declared "With 50 years of hard evidence at hand, it's awful hard to 'slough off' the truth…It's all about PEOPLE![1]" Notwithstanding this observation, there is a common misperception that employee engagement means employee satisfaction. This is a reason why Human Resource issues are often relegated to the end of a meeting, and why Human Resource professionals are often viewed as "too soft."

Engagement is not an end in and of itself – it's not about having things (the best of benefit programs or the highest bonus checks), or even about instituting a training program or a flexible work week. Successful engagement is about creating, incentivizing, and sustaining:

- a learning culture

---

[1] NOVA Documentary, "Peter Drucker: An Intellectual Journey," WGBH TV, Boston, June 2004

- transparent and frequent communication
- the pursuit of high performance; and
- alignment with company and individual goals.

An engaged culture is like a society: when people pull together with a common purpose, both its citizens and its economy will thrive.

For engagement to exist there must be mutual commitment between the employer and employee, wherein the employer is helping the employee reach his or her untapped potential and the employee is helping the employer meet and surpass its business goals.

Engagement is Not a Program

"Programs" are a recipe for bureaucracy – most of us who have worked in offices have seen this happen. However efficient the individuals or the team tasked with implementing a program may be, at some point those individuals have got to get back to the day-to-day routine of making money for the company and for themselves, or the company has to support an administrative layer with an often very narrow focus.

Engagement is a recipe for sustained high performance because it entails a cultural shift – a change in how things are done and how things are communicated from the top to the bottom of an organization. It's no one person's job; it certainly isn't the job of Human Resources or of the CEO alone. Nor is it ultimately the job of any committee or action team. It is an ongoing part of business – and once you embark on systemic employee engagement, there is no finish line. It is a journey without a destination.

Engagement Acknowledges, Then Engenders Optimal Work-Life Balance

A culture of engagement is not based on workaholism. There are companies where it is routine that staff work late into the night, or come in on weekends… all without ever achieving a lift in the bottom line. Somehow or other, consciously or unconsciously, employees manage to regain what they may feel is effort or time being unfairly demanded of them. And if they lack one of the critical earmarks

> **An engaged culture is like a society: when people pull together with a common purpose, both its citizens and its economy will thrive.**

of engagement – the sense that everyone at every level is in this together – there simply isn't much incentive to go above and beyond. They might be putting in the time, but are they putting in the effort?

One of the best definitions of engagement I've seen is from the second edition of *Investing in People*, the bestselling book by Wayne Cascio (with John Boudreau)[2]:

Engagement is a positive, fulfilling, work-related state of mind that is characterized by vigor, dedication, and absorption. Vigor refers to high levels of energy and mental resilience while working, the willingness to invest effort in one's work, and persistence even in the face of difficulties. Dedication is characterized by a sense of significance, enthusiasm, inspiration, pride, and challenge at work. Absorption consists of being fully concentrated, happy, and deeply engrossed on one's work whereby time passes quickly, and one has difficulty detaching oneself from work.

When leaders tell employees where they're going, why they're going there, and how they're going to get there – and when they provide appropriate levels of trust, recognition, and empathy – productivity goes up. I've seen it happen – the chapters that follow will provide many examples. When I moved from a pure HR function to an operations function, I saw the business impact of engagement firsthand. After developing and implementing engagement in the workplace, and monitoring the results, I'm here to tell you that it just makes good business sense.

Employee Turnover Hurts

At the most basic level, employee turnover is expensive. Industry sources tell us that the cost of turnover is somewhere between the annual salary to three times the annual salary of the person who's being replaced. The cost of running ads and/ or commissioning a recruiter is just the beginning; the more difficult and more expensive outlay includes the loss of productivity, while the empty position is unfilled. Also, what about the intellectual property that the person who leaves voluntarily takes with him or her, and the waste of the financial investment a

---

[2]   Cascio, Wayne F. with Boudreau, John. Investing in People. Upper Saddle River, NJ: Pearson/FT Publishing, 2008

company has made in that person? Not to mention the very real likelihood of the disengaged employee leaving your business to join your competitor –meaning you've just donated an advantage to your competition.

The damage doesn't stop there. Turnover has a Pied Piper effect. As people walk, others will talk. And speculate. They'll wonder, "Why did John quit?" Even the sunniest internal communications spin on the situation can't entirely eradicate gossip or skepticism. Even if an employee is leaving on the best possible terms, those who stay are bound to wonder, "What did John know that I don't?" "Should I be looking around, too?" And if the terms of the parting-of-ways are less than ideal, or if people are quitting in droves, the impacts on morale are even more detrimental.

But even in today's economic climate, we're engaging fewer employees than ever before. In a recent Towers Watson study, it was reported that only 24% of today's employees are engaged[3]. This lack of engagement is costing companies billions of dollars in lost productivity and reduced levels of client service, resulting in declining profits and worsening client satisfaction. When the war for talent is intense, there is a point where losing a good employee is worse than losing a good client.

So, why aren't more companies paying attention?

The War for Talent is Not Over

In truth, all people can be replaced. Just look at the revolving door for CEOs of the Fortune 500! When one's inbox is flooded with resumes, it can seem that there's little reason to focus on retention or engagement. But this is a fatal mistake. *Employees who are treated as replaceable are not engaged.* If your company is seeing layoffs or voluntary attrition, DO NOT assume that the people who stay are the truly dedicated employees. Unfortunately, this is rarely the case – and the attitude that people or positions are disposable is tough to disguise. Often, the best and the boldest are those who will risk testing the waters of the marketplace, while those content with their standard contribution to the status quo will go on giving their serviceable, minimal effort.

[3]   Towers Watson 2007-2008 Global Workforce Study

With engagement levels at demonstrable lows and many employees' eyes on the next big break the economy may afford them, there is a real threat that businesses will soon be faced with a staff exodus. The waste – in training and intellectual capital, but also in revenue – will be colossal. A September 2009 study by Deloitte showed 49% of employees are considering leaving their jobs within a year[4].

Shifting Expectations and Drivers

Owing in part to recent economic setbacks, many early Baby Boomers are putting off retirement. This has an effect on succession planning: if the trend continues, we'll be looking at a growing disengagement concern – the "Get Out of My Way" syndrome. The same 2009 Deloitte study cited above finds that only 37% of Generation X plan to stay with their current employers over the next 12 months. I doubt this is a coincidence. Gen X is the generation waiting in the on-deck circle. If Boomers delay retirement and Gen X can't go up, they will go out. What will the fallout be at your firm?

Retirement en masse of a generation renowned for its workaholism is only being forestalled by a few years. It is inevitable. Who is going to fill these seats? The "Baby Bust" generation (so named because of their smaller numbers compared with the "Baby Boom" generation) is coming up now, as are the colloquially-termed Generations X and Y. Much fuss has been made in the press and in business books about how to cater to the differing needs of these diverse groups of employees, and there are of course complexities that bear examination (see Step 5).

How to engage them is at issue, perhaps. *Whether* to engage them is decidedly not.

Companies who view current economic conditions as an excuse to avoid engaging their employees will pay a significant price when the War for Talent resumes. And make no mistake, it will.

Employees are Our Greatest Asset...
and There's This Fabulous Bridge For Sale

There's a reason that humor like Scott Adams's "Dilbert" continues to capture the popular imagination. The experience of dealing with clueless or disingenuous

---

[4]   *Managing talent in a turbulent economy*, Special Report on Talent Retention: Deloitte, September 2009

management has been, perhaps since the inception of the modern workplace, rife with opportunities to make fun. No place of employment is perfect, and missteps, however well intentioned, are going to be scrutinized and, if warranted, mocked. "Dilbert" even spoofed engagement and management in the November 22, 2009 strip depicted below.

This Scott Adams "Dilbert" cartoon appeared in national newspapers on November 24, 2009

The title of this book, *Louder than Words*, is a bit of a poke at the all-too-common practice of paying lip service to employee engagement while continuing with business as usual. This is perhaps the worst mistake of all. Companies who do not pretend to engage their staff are seldom the subjects of Dilbert cartoons. It is the shortfall between the promise and the reality that is laughable, and that often leads individuals to seek employment where that gap is not so broad.

It has been my experience that a work environment, like any other microcosm, has its own highly attuned authenticity detector. If and when your organization realizes the need for engagement – and hopefully this book will help with that transition or enhancement – the change must be embarked upon transparently and sincerely, and communicated constantly and well. There was a time when every employee from the top to the bottom of an organization needed to be able to deliver the company's "elevator blurb —" the pithy summation of what your company does that indicates its overarching vision. Today, your employees should also be able to enthusiastically describe your company's values and culture during that same elevator ride. If your staff are not able to do this, that's a sign of disengagement, and perhaps misalignment as well – an indication that management needs to be communicating better.

A concise and compelling statement or "elevator pitch" is a big plus. The stated purpose of AECOM, a Fortune 500 professional services company specializing in engineering, architecture, design, planning, science and program and construction management, is "To enhance and sustain the world's built, natural, and social environments." This has become a rallying cry for AECOM's 45,000 employees: one that links to the company's internally expressed core values, and that provides direction and meaning.

Communication, of course, cannot be one-way. Calls for feedback cannot be disingenuous, or issued for form's sake only. It's naturally important to manage your message and to respond to vocal skeptics in the right way – see Step 4 for more on this – but it's equally critical to *mean* it when you say that you want to know your employees' opinions... and to follow them up. A company where employees feel comfortable participating in dialogue with anyone, anytime, however senior, is a company well on its way to an engaged culture.

I was reminded of how corporate communication often works (or doesn't work) while running in a 5K race a few years back. The race was a giant "U," with a defined start and finish, and was packed with 12,000 runners at all levels. Given my running prowess (or lack thereof), I was slotted to start at the back of the pack. I only learned that we were off and running by rumor – I never heard the starting gun.

It's probably a sign of how passionate I am about this subject that one of the first thoughts that crossed my mind was how similar the experience was to the way that important information is communicated in a non-engaged company. The CEO and other executives hear the starting gun – or are the ones firing it in many cases – and everyone else is left to follow the general, vague motion forward. Just like the elite runners at the front of the pack, leadership is at the front of the communication pipeline. When an important change is to be communicated, leadership has time

to weigh alternatives, debate options, "sleep on it," and digest the decision. Employees, like myself at the start of the race, are at the back of the pack when they finally receive the communication. And unlike leadership, they often don't have time to properly digest it or consider the alternatives, and they may be unaware of how much time leadership has invested in the decision. When a decision or change is finally communicated, employees ask, "What are they thinking?" and leadership asks, "Why don't they get it!" This fissure is at the root of many communication disconnects in organizations today.

Companies that successfully engage their employees don't allow this to happen. To cultivate an engaged culture, the language of engagement – as well as of every other major company tenet – must become part of the air your employees breathe. The chapters that follow will provide simple, practical methods for cascading the company message and ethos from upper management down through the ranks in ways that are clear, concise, and compelling – and that will result in higher discretionary effort on the part of your employees.

As this book walks through the Ten Steps of Engagement, you will note some common threads: the need for alignment; the vital role one's supervisor plays in the engagement process; and, perhaps most pervasively, the power of communication: the "cornerstone of engagement." A study by Aberdeen Group, a research firm headquartered in Boston, recently noted that firms are beginning to understand the importance of the three engagement pillars depicted on the following page.

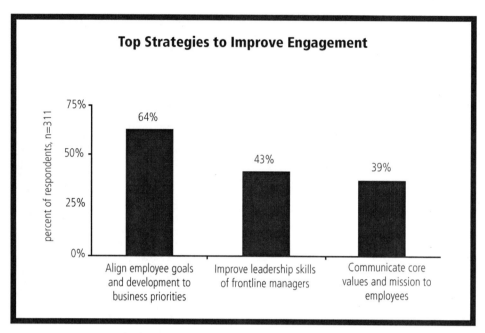

Source: Aberdeen Group, July 2009: *Beyond Satisfaction: Engaging Employees to Retain Customers*

It's About Disengagement, Too.

For years, consultants and academics have talked about the need for employers to engage employees in order to capture their discretionary effort. This is not new. Now, however, addressing disengagement is equally important.

Those who are engaged are increasingly becoming frustrated by their colleagues' disengagement. They're wondering whether their discretionary effort is worthwhile in a climate where they see disengaged coworkers hunkering down to "stay employed." Eventually, they are casting about for a scenario in which their dedication is shared. And when the economic climate is right, they're going to make a move. If you disregard engagement, you may be left with the "disengaged but staying." The same Towers Watson study referenced earlier asked employees who are disengaged if they plan on changing jobs, and remarkably, they report that 15% of disengaged employees have "no plans to leave.[5]" They apparently want to stay and make life miserable for everybody! Companies that allow this to happen will disengage the engaged.

[5]   Towers Watson 2007-2008 Global Workforce Study

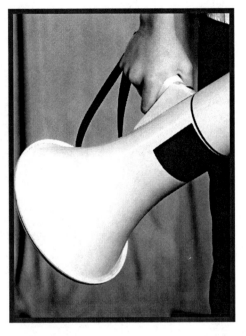

The Ten Steps

In 2009, I established the Employee Engagement Group[6], a division of The Kelleher Consulting Group, to help companies improve their performance through enhanced employee engagement. I began my career as an internal practitioner, developing and implementing successful engagement initiatives for both private and public companies, large and small.

This book contains practical, proven tools that any reader can implement in his or her workplace to combat disengagement and foster engagement. I've written it to ensure that readers can easily pick up and adopt at least one best practice or template or idea per step. The steps are, perhaps, deceptively simple – but that doesn't mean they're easy.

It's always easier just to talk about it. But that's not what this book is about.

[6]   www.employeeengagement.com

Effective leadership is not about making speeches or being liked; leadership is defined by results.

– PETER DRUCKER
Writer, Consultant + Teacher

STEP ONE
THE LINK TO HIGH PERFORMANCE

Employee engagement and profit can seem like difficult metrics to square. One is "soft," having to do with people and their investment in their jobs and their company, and the other is "hard:" numbers. No executive team is going to sign off on a plan to increase employee engagement without some assurance that the Holy Grail – discretionary effort, with its corollary increase in productivity, and ultimately in profit – is a likely result.

To state the case plainly: engagement leads to profit and profit, wisely publicized and distributed, leads to engagement. People want to work for a winner. And in correlating engagement and performance, it should hardly come as a surprise that the employees who go above and beyond – who invest that discretionary effort – are among the most engaged.

It may take time for the two different metrics to square satisfactorily. But having seen effects on the bottom lines of dozens of companies, I can tell you that it's very difficult to have profit without engagement... and that engagement, once established, can see a company through leaner times and help to build it back up. Perhaps surprisingly, a recession or market downturn is not necessarily a bad thing for engagement levels. And you shouldn't be afraid to prune. In fact, given the strong link between poor performance and disengagement, a good place to start might be the aforementioned 15% who are disengaged but staying put! When companies are busy and the job market favors employees, remember that your engaged employees are watching you. You need to keep them engaged without hauling dead weight.

> **Engaged employees are there to GIVE; disengaged employees are there to GET. Low turnover is nothing to boast about if the employees that are staying are disengaged.**

Beware of "Employee Satisfaction to Bankruptcy"

Employee satisfaction is an outcome, not a goal. You may bolster engagement by offering good salaries and benefits, but ultimately the goal is high performance, not satisfied employees. The last thing that anyone wants is a staff populated with satisfied underperformers!

In fact, high performers often become frustrated and disengaged if they see lackluster coworkers receiving the same bonuses or perks that they themselves receive. They will wonder, "Why doesn't management do something about these poor performers?" And regardless of the personal satisfaction they may take in their jobs, they may begin to doubt the judgment and vision of an employer who does not address the discrepancy. I do believe there is a correlation between employee satisfaction and employee engagement. It isn't likely that you would be engaged but not satisfied, although you can be satisfied but not engaged.

Profit is the lifeblood of the organization. And if you lack engagement, gains in profit will be temporary. Conversely, I believe that if you lack profitability over time, engagement levels will drop. Healthy companies sustain both.

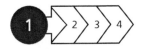

The Right Fit

When I've worked with executives to improve engagement at their companies, I often find that the root of the problem is at the hiring stage. Some companies don't have an engagement problem, they have a hiring problem. The people in charge of interviewing new recruits have to be informed of the company's vision and its employment brand – otherwise they will not be able to articulate the culture to a potential new employee. If you are hiring the wrong cultural fit from the outset, it will be difficult to get those people invested in your organization and working alongside you to achieve your goals. (I'll discuss this in detail in Step 10.)

After all, the vast majority of employees join organizations engaged. You don't hear anyone saying, "I'm joining this company that I hate." But studies show that those initial levels of engagement are not replicated until the seventh year of employment. It takes years for most individuals, who confront a new job with enthusiasm, hope, and considerable personal investment, to find the equilibrium that will incline them to be invested in the greater cause of their organization... and to go above and beyond in their efforts, as they did when they first were hired.

History is filled with companies like Digital Equipment Corporation or Wang Labs who claimed they would never have layoffs. This is not a realistic promise to make, nor should you paint yourself into a corner with such assurances. Firings and layoffs are sometimes necessary. Most employees understand this, and it is far better to be frank about the necessity than to overpromise and underdeliver.

Shortly after my former employer, environmental consulting firm ENSR, embarked on its journey to become an "Employer of Choice," the tragedy of 9/11 put a frost on work in the energy sector, a key client market, resulting in layoffs. Obviously,

> **"They say they want to engage us, but they're letting people go! Sigh. Just more management doublespeak."**

we were concerned that our efforts at engagement would be perceived as hypocritical. But in conducting employee engagement surveys, we learned that on some levels, we'd been almost too sparing in our staff cuts. Our people let us know that allowing mediocrity and poor performance to go unchecked negatively impacted the engagement levels of others. In some cases, it even bred suspicion: "Why does Michael get to stay? Is it because he's friends with the Vice President?" Following the layoff, our Employee Engagement Survey scores actually went up.

High-performing companies identify and act on non-performance before there is an economic reason to do so. Remember – you don't want to be an "Employer of Choice" for mediocrity! The key is to retain and empower the employees who are engaged, and work on the engagement levels of others. If you can't increase the engagement levels of those who are disengaged, you need to be counseling them out of your firm. The true opportunity lies in increasing the engagement levels of the moderately engaged: approximately 71% of your workforce (according to Towers Watson[7]) . If you have high engagement but low profitability, you are much better situated to recover than if you have a staff of satisfied underperformers. A high-profit business with low engagement scores is a mansion built on sand.

Transition Mediocrity… But Love 'Em When They Leave

Clearly, there are emotional reasons to treat people well when you have to let them go. It certainly feels better to lay someone off with a generous severance package and an assurance of endorsement for their job search. But the *real* reason to take care of those you are removing from the company is that it's just good business.

People sue when they're angry. The number of work hours lost in combating a lawsuit, not to mention the cost of any eventual settlement, should serve as a blunt reminder that it's better to make an employee's exit amicable. The dollars invested in modest severance packages don't come close to those potentially at risk in a succession of legal proceedings, even if your company is not at fault.

[7]   Towers Watson 2007-2008 Global Workforce Study

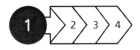

Minimizing resentment and bitterness in a layoff situation is a practical measure in other ways, too. Remember that your employees are watching you. They see how you treat their colleagues and friends, and it effects how they perceive their place of employment. If you have started on the path toward engagement, you have already acknowledged that how you are perceived by your employees matters. This shouldn't stop with the decision to lay someone off.

Every person who is laid off has a network of family and friends. This network could be consumers of your products or services. They could join a competitor – or a far-reaching customer base, like the government. What's more, with the social networking avenues now available, an angry ex-employee now has quick access to a wide array of forums, likely reaching hundreds (and perhaps thousands) of potential customers or clients.

Set and Reinforce High Performance Goals

> On a monthly basis, publicly communicate not only your performance norms, but also your high performance norms. Your staff needs to have a clear picture of what is optimal, not just of the minimum required to get by.

Every company must define its goals and communicate them. Staff at all levels need to know what the goals are, how they will be achieved, and how their individual roles fit into the business strategy. Capture and broadcast performance metrics for staff at all levels, including management. If your organization does not already have a vehicle for soliciting 360-degree feedback in place, institute one. To establish an atmosphere of mutual trust and respect, the executives' performance must be as readily shared as that of any other employee.

Take care in crafting your metrics. Looking at, say, revenue generated per employee will not necessarily give a full picture of why your profitability is rising or falling. If you index such figures against individual performance and engagement surveys, however, you will begin to see a useful pattern.

TOOLS + PROCESSES

LEAP 1 and the Resource Matrix

Over the course of my career, I've conducted countless workshop sessions based on a high performance leadership model called LEAP (Leadership Excellence through Advanced Practices). This four-stage, integrative series of workshops and strategy meetings are designed to engage employees in building a high performing culture, by improving their own performance, and ultimately improving the performance of their department, team, and/or business unit.

Originally, this process was not divided into stages, but was focused more simply on getting managers to identify and further develop their performers, and take action with non-performers. We were seeing that many managers were leading as if everyone was performing at the same level, which clearly was not true. In one case, salary increases were a flat 3% for all employees, regardless of their individual efforts or achievements throughout the year. Surveys, of course, indicated that employees were unhappy with this. Top performers resented the model and became disengaged, and low performers settled into complacency. The result was a culture of mediocrity. We introduced a resource matrix tool, shown below, that encourages leaders to plot employees into one of four quadrants, based on two key criteria: performance and potential.

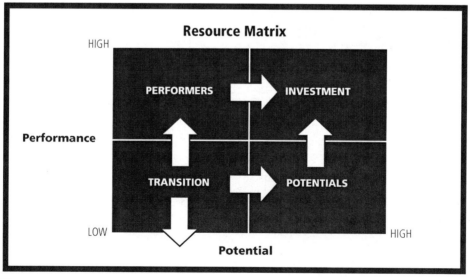

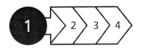

Transition

In this model, transitions (in the lower left quadrant) are not just employees who need improvement, but also new hires and the recently promoted. The inclusiveness of the word "transition" implies (both to the manager and the employee) that this is a temporary state – one which the individual has the power to change. A transitional employee can move in any direction… including right out the front door of a company, if they are not only chronically underperforming but also lack the interest or potential to move to the Performer or Potential quadrants.

Perhaps more than any other aspect of this particular tool, we found that the "transition" label allowed managers to frankly assess their resources… and to handle the sometimes difficult conversations that followed an employee having been identified as a low performer with low potential. In the cases of long-term employees who are categorized as "transition," the tool allows managers to provide solid reasons for the categorization and ask, "How do we work together to move you out of this box?" Hopefully up… but if not, then out.

These conversations are often very productive. But if the answer to the above question is "Nothing," the way forward for the employee is clear… and believe it or not, they may appreciate that clarity.

Performer

Most organizations have a high percentage of employees who are solid performers, but who, for a variety of reasons, aren't showing movement into the "Investment" category. Perhaps their potential to grow is limited by skills, or something more personal, like family, or the desire to limit travel. There's nothing wrong with either of these reasons, or, indeed, with a host of others. Identifying performers whose potential is self-limited often opens up a dialog between manager and employee that is healthy for business. The self-limited employee can continue to perform at a level that is comfortable for his or herself, and the manager can focus staff development resources on employees with the potential to move to the next level of performance.

Potentials

In the lower right quadrant are potentials. These employees are perhaps junior, or have recently been promoted to a new level of responsibility. They exhibit the behaviors and traits of high performance, but because of a lack of tenure, maturity, skill, or knowledge, they aren't yet producing at optimum levels.

These are precisely the employees in whom substantial training dollars should be invested. Perhaps surprisingly, they are also those who need to be challenged with new tasks and asked to shoulder work when times are busy. Why? Both because "potentials" will gain much needed experience from these challenges, and because this strategy avoids burning out your organization's top performers. There's an obvious reason to give tough assignments to the "stars," but if those stars end up over-burdened with work, they may become disengaged. Instead, task your people with potential, wherever feasible.

> To encourage engagement at every level, and to make sure that communication is not solely "top-down," you might follow the example of one California manager I encountered who often asked his most junior staff to lead meetings by sharing the team's scorecard results with the entire office. This powerful idea increased junior staff's engagement levels, and reinforced the importance of business metrics for all members of the office – not just the leadership team. It also was a great developmental opportunity, tying junior staff into the organizational goals.

Investment

These are your stars, and the employees you can least afford to lose. Leadership however, often takes this group for granted. They might pile more and more work on them (after all, they're dependable), and can even limit their career progression ("I don't want to nominate Mary for this position because I don't want to lose her"). Our LEAP model was an opportunity for managers to sit with their stars and inform them they were indeed top performers. (interestingly, this often seemed to come as a surprise) and to map out a more collaborative career plan.

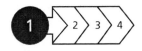

Plotting employees in this way not only allows for a sensible distribution of bonus dollars or salary increases, it provides managers with a clear picture of how to move their people through the quadrants. And it provides a healthy model not just for management but true leadership, which starts with the idea that for optimal results, not every individual should be handled in precisely the same way. It also introduces transparency in performance discussions. If employees are underperforming, shouldn't they know it?

Leverage the Balanced Scorecard

A "Balanced Scorecard" approach to management (See Step 9) has become popular in the last few years. Establishing and communicating your short- and long-term business metrics *in a balanced way* will boost alignment and create line of sight.

Such an approach can assist not only in bolstering a company's mission, but also in engendering employee engagement. Leaders don't only need to know how their staff is performing – they need to know how they themselves are performing. The catch being, of course, that in a truly engaged culture those results must be communicated to the staff at large.

The scorecard process supports an open and communicative culture, and the employee feedback fuels improvements to the company's internal brand. (See Steps 4 and 9 for more on the importance of branding.) In case after case, it's not good enough to simply deploy a balanced scorecard program with the hopes of increasing accountability and engagement at all levels. Employees are watching and listening, and if you don't communicate properly and follow through with results, they are going to notice.

Leadership should be born out of the understanding of the needs of those who would be affected by it.

– MARIAN ANDERSON
Singer

STEP TWO
IT STARTS AT THE TOP

In 2009, I had the privilege to hear Captain Michael Abrashoff, author of **It's Your Ship – Management Techniques From the Best Damn Ship in the Navy,** present at a conference – and he related one of those quiet but standout leadership stories that really illustrate the value of "walking the walk." Abrashoff had just taken over as commander of the aircraft carrier USS Benfold. He was brought in and specifically tasked with turning the morale of the ship around (throughout the US Naval fleet, the USS Benfold had one of the lowest levels of reenlistment – a critical engagement benchmark).

Captain Abrashoff wanted to do away with the perception of special privileges on board his ship. On his very first day, as he stood in the long buffet line for his lunch, one of his officers walked over to him and pointed out that as

Captain, he was eligible to wait in the much shorter line for officers (clearly visible to all the personnel in the eatery).

Abrashoff said, "No thank you, I'll wait in this line with everyone else." After a few uncomfortable minutes, under the eyes of the rank and file, those in the "officer line" began to leave their privileged position and join the longer buffet line.

This powerful day-one metaphor helped Captain Abrashoff break down the class barriers that had been contributing to disengagement aboard the USS Benfold. Over time, under Abrashoff's leadership, the Benfold not only became one of the highest-performing ship in the naval fleet... it also attained one of the highest levels of re-enlistment.

Definition of "Leader" and "Leadership"

In this chapter, I'll address the importance of leadership as a key driver of engagement if employee engagement is to take hold and grow. And by the words leader and leadership, I am talking about roles, whether titled or not, that are distinct from manager and management. Many leaders are managers, of course, but it takes a certain set of behaviors, traits and abilities for a manager to become a leader. I don't mean to denigrate the essential role that management plays in the stability of a company – that would be foolish. In fact, it is critical for leaders to be effective managers as well as effective leaders. But because employee engagement entails a pervasive change in corporate culture, it unfortunately cannot be simply assigned to just any manager or management team. A leader must understand the need for his or her own deep personal commitment to the necessary changes.

> **Managers manage processes, programs, and data. Leaders lead people. Leaders set the direction; managers follow the plan to get there. And while managers are indispensible in creating and monitoring policy, leaders define and uphold an organization's principles. Managers take care of where you are; leaders take you where you're going.**

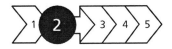

The things that define engagement – trust, clarity, cohesion, collaboration, openness, empowerment, and inspiration, to name a few essentials – are largely the province of an organization's visionaries, role models, innovators, and counselors. These leaders may not be the most senior staff, or hold the loftiest titles or pull down the biggest salaries. But they make their marks on the company culture, inviting multiple perspectives and team decisions while retaining – and communicating – a strong sense of personal accountability.

At the Timberland Company – known for their high-quality boots and other outdoor attire – the link between leadership and the organization's purpose or values could not be more clear. I first met Timberland CEO Jeff Swartz[8] in 2009, when we both participated in a global webinar on corporate social responsibility. He quickly impressed me as a leader who intuitively understood the link between engagement and corporate culture, and I asked to visit the company's corporate offices in Stratham, NH to learn more about Timberland.

I was first struck by the lobby, which seemed dedicated to reinforcing the company's tenacious commitment to social responsibility. Greeting me was a 15-foot-high replica of a boot, primarily remarkable for being made entirely of recycled water bottles. In one corner, stacks of clothing underscored the benefit of using organic cotton in Timberland's products. A sculptural stack of cast-off bicycles provided a visual reminder of the environmental benefits of cycling over driving. Strings of old lightbulbs hung from the ceiling suggested the energy savings possible by replacing three regular bulbs with compact fluorescents[8].

I was introduced to John Pazzani, Timberland's Chief Culture Officer. I asked if everyone at Timberland shared the same values I had sensed in Jeff Swartz, and seen validated by the lobby installation. Kate King, from Timberland's communications group, replied "I think that just about every one of our employees can recite our four core values – Humility, Humanity, Integrity, and Excellence."

As a successful, publicly traded company, Timberland understands commerce and the need to turn a profit. However, in Jeff Swartz's words, "commerce and

---

[8] Timberland's roots go back to 1952, when Nathan Swartz bought into the shares of the Abington Shoe Company. Mr Swartz purchased the balance of the firm in 1955; three generations of Swartzes have run the company since then.

[9] 300 lbs of carbon dioxide a year!

justice must be linked." You can have profitable growth and be committed to the environment, your immediate community, and social justice abroad.

At Timberland, building a company that cares while balancing the needs of shareholders and stakeholders begins with the CEO's personal commitment and demonstration of the firm's values.

Identify a Senior Champion

Often, leaders (including many, many CEOs and CFOs!) are highly analytical, and are more comfortable with hard data. They'll want to know: what are you measuring? What are you reporting to your Board? "Soft" initiatives are rarely intuitive for the very people who need to be "sold on" engagement. As mentioned in Step 1, you will likely need to make the case that engagement and performance, including profitability, are interrelated.

There may be an outside driver that can help make your case – your "burning platform," so to speak. At ENSR, our clients let us know that the level of voluntary turnover was unacceptable – and this, in turn, forced us to take a serious look at the state of engagement within our company. At AECOM and many other firms

during boom times, the war for talent, keeping and finding great staff, was the driver. If a down economy is the burning issue, companies need to continue to see the need to retain and train good people in order to maintain their edge. It is about balancing the needs of today with the sustainability of tomorrow.

Top leaders need to believe in and be able to articulate engagement. But more than that, they need to be held accountable for it.

People are competitive by nature, and how one is being measured is an important driver. Unless a CEO's Board measures a CEO on engagement, there may not be an impetus to lead any differently. Only when senior management is regularly measured and judged on engagement criteria (by reporting on engagement every single quarter, and communicating the CEO's performance metrics throughout the company) will they be motivated to measure up. Having the CEO champion one's engagement efforts makes a difference, as evidenced by Aberdeen Group research shown below.

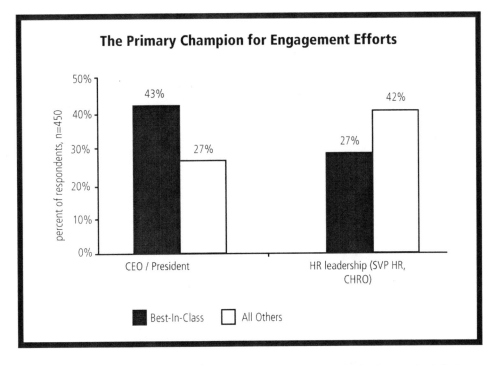

Source: Aberdeen Group, July 2009: *Beyond Satisfaction: Engaging Employees to Retain Customers*

However, because most CEOs are more comfortable working their left brain (analytical, sequential, objective) than their right brain (random, creative, subjective), they may be prone to relegate the primary responsibility for engagement to the HR or communications department, rather than championing the cause themselves. Don't let that happen. If engagement is solely driven by HR, it will likely be perceived by employees as just another "flavor of the month" program. Senior leaders must support engagement to minimize the risk that it is viewed as a touchy-feely, lip-service-only, employee-satisfaction initiative. If the CEO lacks the time or talent to champion engagement, someone else at the senior level most be identified – someone senior enough to give engagement credibility, and, preferably, someone who is perceived as having the "ear" and support of the leader.

Regardless of personal preferences, all senior leaders need to speak the language of engagement and behave in demonstrably committed ways. One of my favorite metaphors for disengagement is the standard parking arrangement in some companies, where the executives get the close-to-the-front door parking while others have to park "out back." This upside-down policy reinforces hierarchy at the expense of trust, investment, and alignment – key elements of engagement. Make no mistake about it – you will have difficulty capturing the discretionary effort of your employees when you have such antiquated visual "perks."

A visible personal commitment to the values of engagement will help your engagement culture. Senior leaders "walking the talk" really works. I recall a business trip where a few executives, including myself and ENSR CEO Bob Weber, were travelling with a new and more junior member of the team. When Bob arrived at the hotel, he was told that he was eligible for a suite. He declined, saying that he didn't need one – but asked the hotel clerk to give it to the most junior team member traveling with us. As the junior employee checked out, and thanked the desk clerk for the upgrade, the desk clerk said, "Don't thank me – thank your CEO. He gave up his suite for you!"

I later learned how this small story took on a life of its own in the company cafeteria. You can't buy or manufacture this kind of "engagement" PR. It fosters trust and the sense that everyone truly is "in this together."

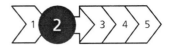

Design and Budget your Engagement Plan

Engagement requires an investment no different than financing a project or new product. According to Boston's Aberdeen Group, "Best-in-Class" organizations[10] are 40% more likely to allocate budget dollars for engagement efforts[11] .If one of your goals is to reduce voluntary staff turnover, you have to beef up your training and retention budgets. Perhaps you need technology to support and track recruitment, or renewed focus on leadership development. You may need to give people stretch assignments, provide a budget for mentoring and cross-training opportunities, fund external training initiatives, or reward outstanding performance via increases to your bonus pool. Remember, money may not motivate people, but the perception of inequity can certainly disengage them.

> During one memorable meeting, an executive voiced an important point to a room full of other executives that has stuck with me: "ENGAGEMENT IS NOT FREE."

Key engagement items such as communication initiatives or talent management systems cost money and must be formally budgeted. And as with any other budget, there must be accountability. Engagement cannot be relegated to a lower place on the budgetary totem pole. A manager might, for example, be temporarily more profitable because s/he is not investing appropriately in development. There are short term financial gains, sure – but if s/he isn't in alignment with the engagement plan, their actions are undermining the message and the vision of engagement, which will ultimately have a long-term business cost. This manager needs to be reminded of the bigger picture, and held accountable.

When you just manage to the bottom line, you might be compromising both engagement and innovation. You need to invest today for both next year and next quarter. Don't be the farmer who eats his seeds instead of planting them.

---

[10] The top 20% of aggregate survey respondents that performed best across three key performance indicators: a) Employee performance (defined as year-over-year improvement in the percentage of employees ranked as "meets" or "exceeds" performance expectations at last performance review); b) Employee referral rates (defined as year-over-year improvement in employee referral rates); and c) Percentage of employees who indicate they are highly engaged (as a result of the most recent employee engagement survey).

[11] *Beyond Satisfaction: Engaging Employees to Retain Customers*: Aberdeen Group report, July 2009.

Link with Strategic Planning Process

You can't accomplish every engagement goal in Year One. There are, of course, other priorities and initiatives needing investment: you might want to acquire another organization, launch a QA/QC system, increase business development, or upgrade your IT infrastructure. You need to prioritize.

One of the challenges many companies face when embarking on an engagement initiative is where to invest first. Surveys are an important tool in determining where you'll get the most bang for your buck. When ENSR first embarked on its engagement journey, for example, one board member suggested we consider doubling the company 401K match to show support for our employees' future. However, our employee engagement surveys did not support this – not one person mentioned the need for an enhanced 401k match. Hundreds, on the other hand, mentioned training and development as a key need, so it became a goal for ENSR to become best-in-class in that arena.

Another excellent example of a senior leader owning (and planning for) engagement is John Chambers, the charismatic and well-known president and CEO of Cisco Systems[12]. Since assuming the helm in 1995, he has been instrumental in positioning Cisco as a leader in its industry and in its corporate social responsibility efforts. (As we'll discuss in subsequent chapters, employees want to work for "companies that care.")

[12] A global leader in Internet networking, with 63,000 employees.

Recently, Chambers commissioned a cross-sectional workforce council focused specifically on employee engagement. This committee was tasked with developing a five-year plan and reporting its progress directly to Chambers and his operating committee. By leveraging his leadership position to demonstrate his personal belief in engagement in a tangible and measurable way, Chambers is effectively "walking the talk." Not surprisingly, in Cisco's most recent employee engagement survey, 99% of its respondents answered in the affirmative when asked, "Do you feel proud to work for this company?"

Keep It Simple and Execute it Flawlessly

You can't do it all. So do an extraordinary job of publicizing your efforts to accomplish your engagement goals over a five-year rolling window, with a

commitment to focus on those top three or four goals for that upcoming year. Reinforce them regularly. Report on your successes. Next year, take on the next three or four priorities. Be frank that engagement is a journey that will evolve over multiple years, and that you can't do it all this year. Employees will understand

that you are running a business and that you have many things to accomplish. Tell them, "This year, we're also going to be investing in (blank). We'll let you know how we're tackling our engagement goals." There is nothing wrong with being transparent about limitations.

All the time you're branding, improving communication, and making employees feel invested because their feedback is helping to determine the priorities (and they are seeing the results).

From the Trenches...

Just as ENSR's culture of engagement got a boost from the simple gesture of relinquishing a fancy hotel room, I've seen other companies' gestures communicate blatant disregard for employees – even when they're talking about engagement at every opportunity. Recently, the general manager of a well-known hotel chain decided to outsource housekeeping. (If individual housekeepers were "lucky" enough to be kept by the outsourcing firm, their wages would be cut in half). The outcry was enormous. Other employees, customers, even the state's governor all banded together, with the governor even asking the public to frequent other hotels instead. The now-embarrassed hotel chain, whose CEO had earlier received a significant bonus, had a PR disaster on their hands.

We all know that bad news travels fast. Well, so does hypocrisy.

The willingness to engage employees in tough decisions, on the other hand, can have widespread benefits. At Boston's Beth Israel Deaconess Medical Center, CEO Paul Levy and his staff faced grave financial hurdles during the recession of 2009.

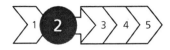

Faced with a $20 million-dollar deficit that might have forced 600 layoffs, Levy asked for alternative recommendations from his employees. Suggestions from staff included suspension of the hospital's 401K match along with several concessions on the part of senior staff: pay cuts accompanied by a freeze on salary increases and bonuses.

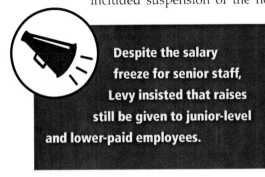

Despite the salary freeze for senior staff, Levy insisted that raises still be given to junior-level and lower-paid employees.

According to Levy, implementing these suggestions was simply the right thing to do to protect jobs in a faltering economy. In addition to communicating effectively on an internal level, Beth Israel Deaconess Medical Center received national media attention[13]. But more importantly, the hospital has seen their $20 million dollar shortfall turn to a $10.3 million surplus, during which time they were able to reinstitute pay increases (and are forecasting a return to their 401K Company match). I would add that they've also positioned themselves as an Employer of Choice in the healthcare market[14].

---

[13]   Kevin Cullen's article "A Head With a Heart," published in the Boston Globe on March 12, 2009 and available on www.boston.com, received among the most positive email responses the site has ever recorded.

[14]   In the spirit of full disclosure: my wife, a two-time breast cancer survivor, received extraordinary treatment at Beth Israel Deaconess Medical Center. I can say from personal experience that at the patient level, one immediately senses employee engagement.

TOOLS + PROCESSES

LEAP 2 and the Communication Commitment

The principles taught in the LEAP workshops (discussed in Step 1) for developing and nurturing high individual performance can also be applied to the performance of teams and business units. The cornerstone of LEAP 2 is to engage employees in designing and owning action plans that serve as local blueprints for business unit or a team's success. Using a performance matrix, each operating unit's profit is plotted on one axis, and its growth on the other.

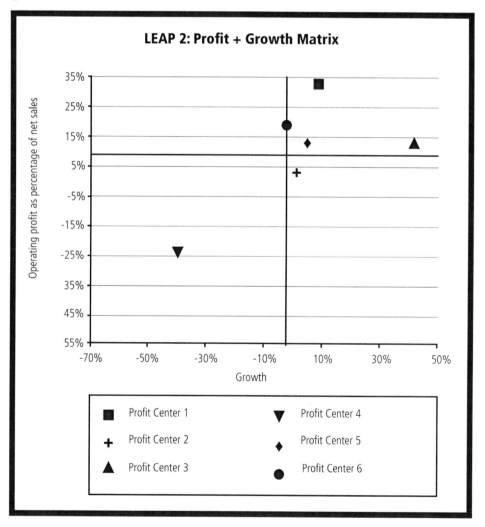

Overall unit performance on both dimensions falls into four performance quadrants, similar to those in the LEAP Resource Matrix discussed in the last chapter, and with similar ramifications. For instance, a unit in the transitional quadrant, which is underperforming, must move "up or out," figuratively speaking, and a cross-sectional team of its managers and employees must develop and implement a plan for improvement. These workshops focus on employees and leaders jointly developing a detailed action plan that addresses "Where are we today?" "Where do we want to go?" and "How do we get there?"

Formalize Reporting and Budgeting

To give engagement its due importance and to reinforce its progress and messages, agendas for operational review meetings must be balanced between profitability and organizational issues and engagement ones. Engagement cannot be shunted to the end of every meeting, where it will stand a higher chance of being given less attention. Similarly, presentations (to the Board of Directors as well as to employee groups at all levels) on engagement goals and progress must be scheduled and systematized, with plenty of time budgeted for questions and discussion.

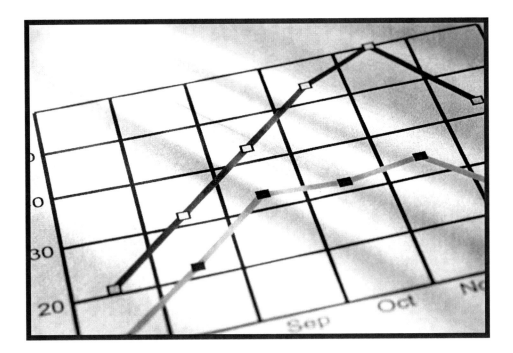

As mentioned above, don't treat engagement as free or even cheap. Create a budget for initial surveys, and use that bottom-up feedback to determine your goals. Just as you would for "hard" programs, formalize your line items and track how your money is being spent. Make adjustments over time as appropriate.

Communication from the Engagement Champion(s)

Your senior leaders (up to and including the president/CEO/COO/CFO) must be upholding their responsibilities in communicating the business strategy every month... especially with regards to how engagement fits in. This communication can take the form of a newsletter, an email, a report, a video, or a presentation, but don't let it fall by the wayside in favor of just "hard" topics like profitability or M&A.

Engagement Workshops

As you are determining the strategic investments you will make, you will need to enlist everyone in your organization to attain an accurate picture of where you will get the most "bang for your buck." Surveys are an indispensible tool, as are one-on-ones or brown bag sessions with travelling executives. However, to reinforce the message that engagement is important, training sessions on leading an engaged workforce are practical ways to get people leaders up to speed on how their style of management may need to shift. (See Step 4 for more on these workshops.) Such sessions are an excellent arena to roll out the Communication Commitment (discussed in Step 7) or other tools. They also provide yet another opportunity for feedback and dialogue between management levels, and are in and of themselves a step toward engagement in that they allow staff to participate fully in determining top-line engagement goals.

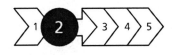

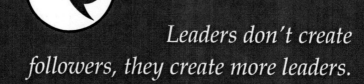

*Leaders don't create
followers, they create more leaders.*

– TOM PETERS
Writer

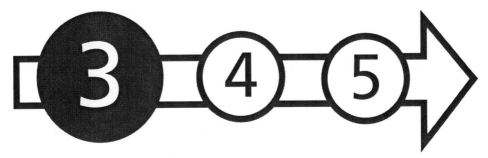

STEP THREE
ENGAGE FIRST-LINE LEADERS

The Engagement Impact of the First-Line Supervisor

If you are looking to make employee engagement a pillar of your company, you very likely have an underused (and very important) regiment – your first-line managers. Countless studies reinforce that one of the top engagement drivers is first-line leadership; these are the people who can truly make or break your efforts because they are perfectly positioned to transmit key information up and down the ranks. What drives a given individual to excel or to become complacent? It's the responsibility of his or her immediate supervisor to find out.

On the flip side, disengaged managers are, on average, three times as likely to have disengaged direct reports[15].

[15]   Sirota Survey Intelligence Inc. study, 2009

It's an old adage that in my many years of experience I have yet to see disproven: people join great companies, but leave bad managers. Clearly, if your first-line leaders are not in alignment with your company's engagement goals, your chances of success are slim to none.

For many years, I've found it ironic that the employees who need the most care – entry-level staff – are entrusted to managers who have, on average, the least experience, and who are often lacking in the very communication skills that are required to establish trust and create alignment. On the other side of the spectrum, senior leaders who have honed their communication skills over the years, and have accumulated many years of practice in leading people, are most likely directing senior executives who are self-sufficient and independently motivated. Think about it – junior staff, who are dependent on others, and are being led by first line managers who are the least experienced and perhaps least capable in the leadership "food chain." In other words, those who have the skill are leading people with nominal need, while those who lack the required skills and experience are leading those with the greatest. This attenuation of leadership traits at the first line-manager level can be a tremendous stumbling block to engagement that requires ongoing training and monitoring.

The biggest guns in the engagement arsenal are people-leaders who *actually have the ability to lead people and create follow-ship*. Many line managers achieve their position for the wrong reasons: tenure, technical ability, and personal ambitions, chiefly. And unfortunately, the ability to lead people is a trait that almost everyone thinks they've got! Those who would never venture an opinion on a technical issue may have completely misplaced confidence in their communication and team-building skills, for example. This hindrance to engagement is magnified by the fact that very few line managers are being assessed on their people skills as a core competency, let alone as a requirement for advancement. One of the biggest mistakes companies make is to assume that an outstanding employee is also an outstanding succession candidate. For instance, many great salesmen make lousy sales managers.

If you don't make engagement a job requirement, and measure one's effectiveness in engaging their staff, your line managers won't find the time to do it. They're

being asked to do so many other things; they need to be trained in, and evaluated on, leading people, A key first step to build engagement with your first line leader is to treat him or her as part of the leadership of the company, including making sure that even first line leaders receive critical communication in advance of the general population. They need to learn the issue, policy change, or strategic plan thoroughly, including what has already been challenged or debated, and they need the opportunity to ask questions of their own. They may need time to digest a policy change and to think through how to incorporate it into their group's work. Most of all, they must appear informed when they transmit the information to their staff. Otherwise, their authority is diminished, and they will have a difficult time showing genuine support of the new information. They may become cynical... and cynicism at the line-manager level is arsenic in the engagement well.

Line managers must also be told that in taking on responsibility for leading people, they forfeit the right to vocal cynicism. At ENSR, as we were working toward the goal of becoming best-in-class in health and safety, we needed to ensure that all of our field people were adequately trained and always wearing the correct safety gear. It came to our attention that one line manager was not only refusing to take our goal seriously – he was actually communicating his opinion that the entire project was unneccessary.

> As Timberland's Chief Culture Officer John Pazzani says, "We don't care if someone is a great accountant. He or she is not going to be an accounting supervisor unless they exhibit leadership traits that are consistent with Timberland's four core values: humility, humanity, integrity, and excellence."

Allowing this sort of misalignment at the line-manager level undermines engagement. To attain or retain a line management role, it must be understood that success does not only mean keeping the numbers up. It means providing hope, guidance, inspiration, and vision. If your first-line leaders disagree with a corporate mandate, they need to discuss this with those above them, and not express their displeasure with those below.

Take a hard look at your organization. Who are your best managers of people? What are the behaviors and traits that make them so good? It can't simply be that they're easy to work for, obviously – their teams have to be held accountable for their performance or non-performance.

Make a list of your discoveries. These are the behaviors and traits that define success in your firm, and the traits you must cultivate in each and every line manager. Be prepared to make an investment in the development of people skills in the same way you would in technical skill development. This critical subject will be discussed in much more detail in Step 10.

The Importance of 360-Degree Assessment for all "People Leaders"

In recent years, drawbacks of the traditional one-on-one review, with the manager as the sole assessor and judge of an employee's performance, have become more widely acknowledged. Companies seeking to improve engagement would do well to explore one popular alternative: the 360-degree review, which not only provides a more balanced view of a person's performance, but can also build trust and strengthen lines of communication between management and staff. However, in a non-trusting culture, the introduction of a 360-degree feedback tool will be met with resistance. It will take time to build organizational support (and trust) before this communication enhancement is embraced.

In a traditional performance review, it is taken for granted that both the reviewer and the reviewed share the same perception of the employee's job requirements and the same understanding of what is meant by "good" or "poor" performance. Rather than treating the review conversation as a means of learning what drives an individual to excel, managers are constrained (and often further handcuffed by ratings systems) to simply informing each direct report how he or she is measuring up to the job as the manager understands it. This is not the sort of conversation that

typically gets at what truly motivates an individual, and without this knowledge, management cannot expect more than a nominal improvement in performance.

A 360-degree review, skillfully applied, is much more revealing. Typically combining self-review with anonymous feedback from everyone surrounding the individual (peers, supervisors, direct reports, and even clients), these reviews provide a picture of how a person's skills and demeanor are experienced by others, and often capture important aspects of performance (such as collaboration with colleagues from different departments) that a traditional review would miss. Instead of simply distinguishing between the excellent, the deficient, and the mediocre, a 360-degree review captures valuable feedback about an employee's behaviors and traits, past performance, developmental needs, and strengths.

There must, of course, be parity in the reviewing process throughout an organization – an idea at which some leaders balk. 360-degree feedback is of special importance for first-line managers because in addition to learning how they are assessed by colleagues and superiors, they learn about how they are leading from those who are being led. Not only does the opportunity to comment on a manager's performance bolster the review process's credibility, it also fosters engagement by demonstrating to junior staff that their experiences matter and that their opinions are important.

360-degree reviews of line managers have two important implications beyond the above in terms of engagement. First, they can reveal to those managers whether or not they are leading in a manner consistent with organizational norms. Second, they can reveal to higher leadership whether or not alignment between the company's overall goals and those of an individual department.

"Leading an Engaged Workforce" Workshops

As part of our early engagement efforts at ENSR, we developed and delivered a series of workshops that were initially designed to address the high level of burnout we were seeing throughout our staff. For years, client satisfaction had been the be-all end-all, superseding all other needs: work-life balance, staff development, and even innovation. Ironically, the result was client dissatisfaction: as some employees left the firm, the clients were negatively impacted by turnover. Clearly, something had to change.

It's important to note that the renewed focus on "people leadership" as a way to build engagement was a non-negotiable obligation on the part of management, in whatever location or at whatever level the individual leader might be. After all, if a company is saying that engagement is part of its culture, people have to be led in a consistent way. I compare it to a prevalent American haircutting chain's appeal. I'm a busy person; I travel a lot, and my schedule doesn't often allow me to keep an appointment at a salon. But I know that if I walk into a Supercuts in Vermont, I'm going to get more or less the same haircut I'd get if I were in a Supercuts in Minneapolis. This consistency in haircutting is part of their business model; consistency in leadership should be part of yours.

Another excellent example of a firm ensuring consistency in leadership practices is General Electric. At the John Welch Leadership Center in Crotonville, New York, all General Electric leaders (whether they work for GE Energy, GE Capital, NBC, Universal, etc.) are all trained to lead in the GE way.

It's not robotic – in Step 5, we'll discuss how to individualize engagement based on the motivational drivers of your employees. But if you have decided, say, that staff

development is to be part of your company's commitment to its employees, and have instituted a company university in support of that goal, it isn't acceptable to have one manager who decides to disregard his staff development goals.

Naturally, your leadership training has to evolve to keep up with organizational needs. At ENSR, we made sure that all of our engagement workshops were focused on those competencies and goals we were looking to reinforce – and fluid enough that our emphasis could change. For instance, early on we included work/life balance and communication modules in our workshops, but over time, these behaviors became embedded in our culture. Subsequent workshops replaced these modules with new needs – innovation and tailoring leadership to different generations' drivers. The workshops became a forum to share organizational best practices, and soon were anticipated by staff as a highlight of working for our company.

Incidentally, I continued to deliver these evolving workshops, even as I became COO (thus reinforcing Step 2). I believe now that the workshops had an additional benefit: they demonstrated that ENSR's investment in its people – foregoing billable hours for two days to make sure that our employees were being led in a consistent manner, whether they resided in Chicago, Hong Kong, or Rio de Janeiro.

From the Trenches...

Throughout this book I talk about the importance of communication; in fact, it is the common thread that links all ten steps together. Like people-leadership, communication is one of those skills at which everyone thinks they're proficient – which can lead to oversights such as the rather embarrassing one I'm about to relate.

I was once on an airplane with a subordinate, on my way to deliver a presentation that included a section on the importance of knowing individual employees' motivational drivers. (The Manager's Desk Reference, refining psychological theory for business purposes, defines these roughly as *achievement, autonomy, safety, affiliation, esteem, authority,* and *equity*[16].)

---

[16]   Adapted from Berryman-Fink, Cynthia and Fink, Charles B. The Manager's Desk Reference. New York, NY, AMACOM: 1989, 1996

"So," my travelling companion asked, "What do you think my main motivational driver is?"

As her supervisor, it was my responsibility to know. But I found myself racking my brain – is she motivated by security? By recognition? Does she love being part of a team? Is she driven by achievement? Eventually I guessed, and I was wrong. I'd taken for granted that because this was my area of expertise, I would somehow have an intuition what drove my people! I ought to have been the one asking the question and initiating that conversation. All leaders should.

This is particularly important during the review process. It's critical not only to ask "What do you want to do?" but "Why do you want to do it?" If you only ask the

first question, you may not get an honest answer – especially if a salary increase is in the offing.

You have to listen, too. I once gave a workshop in which we reviewed 360-degree feedback on each leader present, and noticed that one individual had some of the lowest scores I'd ever seen. Perplexed, I sought the man out in private and asked him about the results. His answer? "See? I told them I didn't want to lead people!"

This person had no interest or aptitude for being a people leader. He was a technician who took great pride in his work, and who had been promoted for all the wrong reasons. He was unsurprised that his staff hated his leadership style – he hated leading!

TOOLS + PROCESSES

360-Degree Performance Feedback Form

There are a number of highly sophisticated 360-degree assessment tools on the market. Some are lean and workable, while others have become bogged in complexity. The tool below is one I've used in the past with great success. It is not overly complicated, takes a few minutes to complete, and can be administered as a simple electronic attachment, or customized by IT specialists (internal or external) to be fully automated.

Employee Being Evaluated: _____

Review Period: From _____ **to** _____

Return To (Current Supervisor: _____

Return By (Date): _____

Your Relationship To Employee Being Evaluated:

☐ External Client   ☐ Internal Client   ☐ Peer   ☐ Direct Report   ☐ Other:

You are being asked to provide input on the employee listed below for an upcoming employee performance and development discussion. Your assessment of his/her performance will ensure a more complete assessment and help to identify strengths and improvement areas. Your input will be anonymous; only composite feedback will be shared with the employee. Return the completed form to current supervisor in a sealed envelope marked "Confidential."

Describe the employee's strengths and improvement areas. Be as specific as possible, including examples.

Strengths:

Improvement Areas:

Assess the employee on the below Behaviors, Skills, and Competencies below. Place an X in the column to provide your rating. If the employee is in a leadership or project management role, also provide ratings of his/her performance on the applicable skills/competencies.	Excellent	Strong to Very Strong	Good	Some skill, not a strength	Minimal
Core Behaviors, Skills + Competencies					
Customer Satisfaction – Performs with (internal or external) client satisfaction in mind, while not compromising the integrity of the work. Identifies client needs and manages the relationship to the benefit of the client.					
Technical Competence and Knowledge – Keeps abreast of new developments in field. Respected and sought out as resource. Enhances professional/technical skill in others.					
Quality – Incorporates quality standards into existing operations. Ensures that work delivered to client meets all standards.					
Productivity – Completes expected volume of work that meets quality standards in time allotted. Willingly works on multiple and additional assignments, when required. Uses time wisely.					
Initiative – Self-starting, resourceful. Searches for new ideas. Sense of urgency about next step. Learns new skills, cross-training, taking coursework, etc. Explores new ways of applying existing resources.					
Communication – Has written and oral skills to effectively perform job responsibilities. Clearly expresses thoughts, ideas, and concepts to subordinates, peers, supervisors, and clients. Listens effectively.					
Planning and Organization – Budgets and uses time effectively. Follows through on work in a timely and cost effective manner. Effectively schedules people and resources to meet goals, making wise use of others' time.					
Dependability – Work requires minimal follow-up. Follows through on commitments. Assignments are completed by deadline.					
Teamwork – Works effectively as team member. Applies tact and courtesy in dealing with others. Promotes cooperation and works effectively with other departments, client service centers, regions.					

Complete this section only if the employee is in a leadership or project management role. Provide ratings of his/her performance on the applicable skills/competencies below.

Managerial Leadership Behaviors, Skills + Competencies	Excellent	Strong to Very Strong	Good	Some skill, not a strength	Minimal
Leadership - Respected and trusted by peers and direct reports. Guides others to work toward common objectives. Acts as positive example to others in supporting company values, mission, and strategy. Has positive impact and is an encouraging influence on others. Seeks feedback to enhance leadership skills.					
Goal Setting – Creates and communicates personal and group vision. Establishes and communicates developmental goals. Enlists support of employee network to pursue goals. Responsive to developmental feedback given by employees.					
Communications – Holds regular meetings to convey corporate and local information. Pursues employee concerns through to resolution. Solicits feedback.					
Mentoring/Employee Development - Develops employees through mentoring, coaching, training, and challenging assignments. Sets clear performance standards. Provides effective annual written evaluation and professional development plan in a timely manner. Offers spontaneous evaluation/feedback on a regular basis.					
Motivation – Provides positive feedback when deserved. Gives public recognition when appropriate. Shows appreciation to dedicated employees and for tasks well done. Bases incentive pay fairly. Moves quickly in confronting issues and resolving problem employees. Seeks employee input.					
Quality and Risk Management: Ensures compliance with quality system and procedures. Evaluates, monitors, and mitigates project risks. Assigns qualified talent to projects. Conducts regular and effective project reviews.					

(Continued on next page)

Complete this section only if the employee is in a leadership or project management role. Provide ratings of his/her performance on the applicable skills/competencies below.

Project Management Behaviors, Skills + Competencies	Excellent	Strong to Very Strong	Good	Some skill, not a strength	Minimal
Project Performance - Meets project requirements through problem resolution, budgeting, resource planning, scheduling, and tracking timely delivery of quality work product within budget. Looks outside of the local business unit to find and use the right talent for the job.					
Business Development - Is active in development and/or implementation of business development plans. Effectively interfaces with clients. Is effective in identifying and developing new and repeat business.					
Financial Management - Demonstrates success in budgeting, resource allocation, cost control, and profit contribution. Manages backlog, bookings, write-offs. Works with line management to schedule work and staff to optimize company utilization.					
Client Relations – Behaves in a professional, positive manner. Manages client relationship as a partnership geared to future business. Ensures that project team is responsive to client. Maintains positive client relationship without jeopardizing Company's financial position relative to the project.					
IAdministration – Completes all project documents on time and files with regulatory agencies, the client, and company management as required. Follows Company records management standards and procedures. Manages time spent on administrative tasks efficiently.					
Participation in Alliances or Major Programs – Gives program assignments proper priority. Understands and adheres to programmatic requirements and procedures. Actively participates in program events.					

Please return completed form to current supervisor in sealed envelope and mark "Confidential." Supervisors will keep this form in a separate file, not with the employee's Employee Development Plan documentation.

Reviewer's Signature (Optional): _____

BEST Profile

Although people are often hired or promoted because of their education and skills, in my nearly 30 years of experience, I have learned that this is the wrong focus. Having the education and skills to do the job is the bare minimum. The most engaged employees (and the best leaders) are engaged because of an inherent set of behaviors and traits they possess – those that define high performance for a particular position.

The BEST Profile			
BEHAVIOR	**EDUCATION**	**SKILLS**	**TRAITS**
How one acts or reacts to specific circumstances	The information a person carries with him or her	The ability to put information into action	Characteristics that define one's personal nature

Strong people skills transcend technical capability. It is possible to successfully lead engineers, for example, without being one. The challenge facing many companies is that salaries and "rank" increase based on individuals' ability to leverage others to get things done. That's why upper managers make more money. In part because of this, a lot of people have aspirations to become leaders of people. But that doesn't mean everyone's good at it.

For true leadership, the necessary competencies go well beyond technical aptitude. Take the time to define the common attributes of the top 10% of your work force (and/or of your most engaged employees). More likely than not, you will discover a common set of attributes that define top performance for your firm. Next, look for others in the company who possess these traits, and consider them your candidates for future line management positions. Also, incorporate these traits into your staff selection criteria when recruiting from outside the company.

If you doubt the efficacy of evaluating your managers in this way, ask yourself whether you've ever fired anyone because s/he lacked education and skills. Now ask yourself whether you've ever let someone go because of a certain behavior or trait.

The same question can be asked for the other side of the spectrum – people you've promoted in the past. It is likely that the promotion was driven by your positive evaluation of the individual's behaviors and traits, and not based on skill or education.

Starting the Conversation

Once you have a clear idea of the behaviors and traits necessary for your organization's first-line leaders, these can serve as the backdrop for performance reviews and other conversations where the subject of promotion to management may arise. Ultimately, you want to enter into a dialogue that will reveal what drives the individual in question, and ideally, you will have been previously acquainted with their behaviors and traits via 360-degree feedback. One tool I have found consistently useful is based on three very simple "needs domains:"

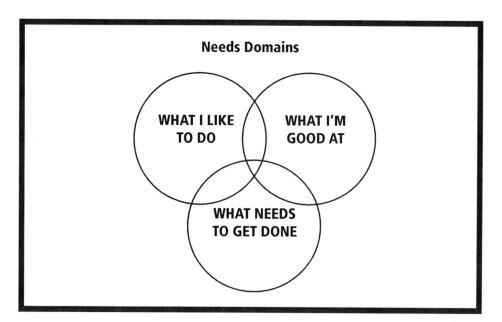

The more you can overlap these three domains, the higher the probability you have an engaged employee. What a person enjoys may not always entirely coincide with what s/he excels at doing. A great example is my golf game – I love playing golf, but hard as I try, I do not excel at it (or as my three life long golf buddies would say, "You stink at it"). Conversely, I don't particularly enjoy cranking through

spreadsheets (don't like to do). But for whatever reason, I seem to have an aptitude for it.

To feel truly engaged, most people need some of each in their jobs. What the organization needs done is the reason the job was created in the first place – the review conversation provides the opportunity to examine how the individual's passions and skills best can be put to work in service of those goals.

An organization needs talented, skilled leaders of people at the line manager level. If a person does not like to lead people or is not currently good at it, they should not be in line for promotion. It's that simple.

I have always found the leadership summary below to be invaluable, and kept it posted on my wall.

Eleven Needs a Leader Must Fill		
1.	Authority	"Someone's in charge."
2.	Security	"Things will probably turn out OK."
3.	Direction	"Someone knows where we're going."
4.	Vision	"We know where we're going.
5.	Structure	"Everybody knows where they fit in."
6.	Clarity	"Someone tells us what's expected of us."
7.	Role Model	"We have someone to look up to."
8.	Reassurance	"Someone's looking after us."
9.	Cohesion	"We're all singing from the same song sheet."
10.	Inspiration	"We feel good about what we're doing."
11.	Recognition	"What I do matters."

The single biggest problem in communication is the illusion that it has taken place.

– GEORGE BERNARD SHAW
Playwright

STEP FOUR
COMMUNICATION – THE CORNERSTONE
OF AN ENGAGED CULTURE

Every company would like to capitalize on the potential benefits of employee engagement, but few executives and managers grasp the full investment required in terms of culture shift and in communication. Employers won't realize the gains of engagement without first acquiring full staff investment in the company. And you can't get full staff investment without making engagement part of your corporate brand.

The terms "brand" and "branding" have suffered from overuse in corporate vocabulary recently. But to go back to Marketing 101 for a moment, it's important to note that when we talk about "brand," we aren't referring simply to your company's logo or tagline, or to the promises it makes to its customers or clients, or to its place and stature in the marketplace. One of the better definitions of "brand" that I've heard is: "a collection of perceptions in the mind of the consumer." I would be inclined to take this one step further and say that a brand also involves the *emotional resonance* of those perceptions.

What does branding have to do with engagement? More than you may think.

We've talked about the ability, willingness, and zeal on the part of employees to deliver your company's "elevator pitch" as important hallmarks of engagement. Essentially, what your people are doing in that brief spiel is **communicating your brand**, and obviously this is vital to the pursuit of new business, new recruits, or potential collaborative relationships. However, the need to instill your brand in your employees does not begin and end with how they speak with people on the outside – your customers, clients, recruits, and business peers. In fact, those audiences may be "1b" priorities for your message.

What and how employees communicate with one another is "1a." In the mini-society of the workplace, attitudes (whether good or bad) are infectious. Confusion, cynicism, disinvestment, and apathy may not be communicated verbally, but if they are part of your company's atmosphere, everyone's breathing the same stale air. If your brand has negative connotations internally, you have an uphill battle ahead of you in getting your employees engaged. They are the first line "consumers" of your message, and their perceptions and emotional responses are profoundly important.

To cite one example, I recall reading an article many years ago about a study of U.S. companies that were striving to determine the front runners in terms of employee benefits programs. To do this, the researchers assessed and compared two data streams: the facts and figures of the programs themselves, and employee surveys designed to evaluate how staff themselves gauged and ranked their companies' benefits.

The results were surprising, although you may have guessed their characteristics by now. The employee survey results bore no relationship to the metrics of the actual benefits programs themselves. In case after case, the companies that excelled at internally promoting the benefits they offered were more highly regarded than

those that offered quantifiably "better" programs. In other words, the companies that *branded* their benefits – that created emotional resonance with the experience of those programs in their staff – were the winners.

Communicate: We Must Win Together

It's important to remember that employees want to work for a winner. Just as they want to be able to sing the praises of their company's innovation, creativity, significance, and market position, they want to be proud of how successful their workplace is in inspiring them, supporting them, and keeping them fired up. This

is an important link between company and employee goals, and if you can capitalize on it, you are well on your way to an engaged culture.

The message must be that "we are all in this together." You need to communicate your objectives and goals often, and report on your progress. If having an engaged culture is an objective (and I hope I'm making the case that it should be), you need to communicate this to your employees and reiterate it at every opportunity, using whatever vehicles are available (newsletters, weekly meetings, email signatures, social media, letters and memos from upper management, etc.). Don't worry about seeming redundant. A communications consultant once told me that in this era of email, text messages, online forums, blogs, and Twitter, employees need to hear or read something 13 times before they absorb it. (And, as an aside, I've never heard of anyone who quit a company because there was too much communication. Have you?)

Clarity, Transparency, Measurement, and Accountability

Whether the message is explicitly about engagement or not, leaders need to tell employees where the company is going as a whole; why it's going there; and how it's going to get there. (And in a truly engaged culture, leaders establish a venue in which their employees have a voice in determining both the path and

the destination.) These goals have to be shared at every level, from corporate through district through region through office through individual line manager. If goals aren't frequently stated and widely known, updates on progress are meaningless. If, for example, your company has six key elements in its strategic plan, simply circulating the plan itself will not incline employees to invest in it. Each person needs to know how his or her job fits into the plan, and what results at each milestone will constitute success or failure. Enlightened companies weave the key elements of their strategic plan into the firm's performance appraisal/employee development process, to create and maintain a "line of sight" from individual positions toward the company's goals.

Business is Not T-Ball

Many companies or managers are hesitant to communicate news of setbacks or losses, fearing that they will contribute to demoralization. In fact, almost the reverse is true. In order to feel invested, employees need to know how the business is doing in relationship to its goals. I frequently remind managers, "Business is not T-Ball," to reinforce the hard fact that companies need to make money. If employees have a sense of how their efforts contribute to the greater good, news of the overall state-of-the-company will produce a "How can I help?" outlook when things aren't going well, rather than simply "How can I benefit?" when they are.

I've often found it ironic that some managers in underperforming business units or departments, having participated wholeheartedly in workshops I've led and digested the 360-degree feedback that is part of the process, are reluctant to move on to the critical next step: sharing the actual results with employees. "We don't want to demoralize our staff!" they exclaim.

We could characterize this concern as retrograde, or perhaps more charitably as protective or paternalistic. But these judgments miss the point: you simply can't get to engagement without honest communication. Imagine a sports team whose players were kept in the dark about whether they were winning or losing, or where no one knew how the team ranked in relationship to its opposition. Would you expect them to improve?

Employees need to know whether their business unit or department is ahead of the curve, on par, or falling short of its goals. If a business is only on par, or average, I am a strong supporter of identifying high performing business units or departments and sharing the relevant internal benchmarks and best practices. Remarkably, (perhaps because of pride) many leaders do not want to reach out to high performing business units within their own companies to ask for advice or assistance. If this is the case, interchanges facilitated by internal or external practitioners are a safe way to share high performing norms without managers' having to ask for advice or help. To stand the test of time, an engagement plan must provide a means by which performance is candidly addressed. Again, employees want to win. No one wants to be considered average. You can't improve if you don't know you're underperforming.

Cascading the Message

No one individual, committee, or department can be placed in charge of disseminating information throughout the company, although of course there are many highly skilled professionals out there who can do a world of good in keeping the communications gears greased and in finding creative ways to broadcast and publicize individual messages. To be sure, communication starts at the top, with the CEO, president, or other appropriate executive. But in order for clear communication to become part of your brand and your corporate culture (and make no mistake, this is absolutely critical for engagement to take hold), there must

be a process by which the message is reinforced by every level of management. The goal is to create parity and alignment between what the CEO is saying and what the line manager is telling his or her direct reports.

This takes time, repetition, and leveraging of available communication options. It also requires acknowledgement that while certain people are better communicators than others, this does not diminish anyone's responsibility. Those for whom consistent, frequent, and genuine communication do not come easily must be given the tools and processes to succeed, and held accountable regardless of their personal preferences or "comfort zones." It is important to point out that all line managers, defined as "people who manage people," have a communication responsibility.

For every charismatic Steve Jobs at the helm, there are probably ten introverted Bill Gateses. But this is not to say that personal charisma is the be-all-end-all of great leadership – otherwise Microsoft would hardly be the industry giant it has become. Indeed, there are plenty of examples in every field (even politics) where

quiet brilliance and a keen business sense has served better than any amount of charm, or eloquence. Jim Collins reinforces this premise at great length while defining his "Level V leader" in *Good to Great*[17]. Still, in successful enterprises of all scales you will more often than not find that leaders who know communication is not their strongest suit still find ways to leverage their talent to disseminate "big messages" at all levels. It takes a bit of humility, but smart CEOs and presidents know that what they themselves may not be able to articulate in the most compelling way can gain power as it percolates through the ranks of the passionate.

> At ENSR, my passion for developing employee engagement at our firm eventually led to my being left "in charge" when the president was on vacation. It's hard to think of a better demonstration of commitment to engagement than putting the "Chief People Officer" in the number two position.

The good news is that while upper management is where the buck stops (or the message starts), in a cascaded communications strategy the responsibility for communication is shared across every level, from the region to the district to the office to the line manager. In such an environment, the opportunity for staff to hear individual messages is greatly amplified. The key is to make every leader a message ambassador, and every management level responsible for informing the next.

I've seen many organizations where the CEO kicks off the message, but then the Human Resources and/or internal communication department carries it forward, ensuring that the ambassadors are informed and actively spreading the word while the leader returns his or her attention to profitability and revenue growth. If you are worried that communication will add to the workloads of already harried line managers, the answer is to equip them with the information and tools that they need to be effective message ambassadors, and let them know precisely what is expected: parity with, and wide and frequent distribution of, the top-line message.

[17]   Collins, James C. Good to Great. New York, NY: HarperCollins, 2001

Finding Disciples... and Disarming Skeptics

At ENSR, when we made the first serious moves toward making engagement part of our culture, we debated whether to tell our employees what our end goal was. We'd decided we wanted to be an "Employer of Choice," and clearly we had work to do to get there. We knew our programs weren't going to be perfect, and we worried that cynicism might trump our efforts. After all, if we had been in our audience's shoes, we might be skeptical too. "Empty promises," "We've heard this before," "Another program," we imagined doubters saying.

Thankfully, we came to our senses. We realized that we were embarking on a multi-year journey, and that if we were truly committed to bringing engagement about, we were going to have to express exactly what we were trying to do and why. We were going to have to report on milestones, whether or not we were proud of the results. We were going to have to make ourselves accountable – that was the only way we could command the respect and trust of the very people we needed to make our culture shift a success.

As we expected, skepticism was a big part of the initial reaction. But because upper management had already been its own harshest critics, this didn't take us by surprise or daunt our resolve. We stuck to the plan. Our CEO, Bob Weber, made employee engagement one of the eight key elements of his strategic plan, and issued monthly progress reports. He wasn't alone. All 10 members of the leadership team spoke continually about employee engagement and were committed to its success. They became true ambassadors of an employee-focused culture.

We kept ourselves accountable both internally and externally. As part of our marketing efforts, we ran a full-page ad, pictured on the opposite page, in the leading trade journal titled: "How about a CEO who reports his progress to you every month?"

We also welcomed criticism and dealt with it in a transparent manner, and in some ways this in and of itself helped to defuse the more vocal skeptics. It's hard to maintain a sour outlook when you're clearly being heard, and when management is openly "fessing up" to missteps and seeking ways to correct the course. The most leathery of skeptics has to concede evident effort on the part of management, and cannot deny it when gains, however small, are being made.

Again, the key is communication. Skeptics who continue to grumble in the face of clear progress and ongoing, frank exchanges between management and staff will quickly find themselves without an audience.

Of course, if your company is like most, there is an existing range of engagement levels throughout your staff. Your most engaged might be your newest recruits (who are full of enthusiasm and eager to prove themselves) or your long-term veterans (who have seen the

good, the bad, and the ugly). If you are fortunate enough to have employees who are visibly committed to your cause, by all means find out *why*. What do they have in common? And how can they help to propagate engagement throughout your organization? In Chapter 10, we'll discuss the importance of identifying the common traits that define your highly engaged employees, and how to identify like traits in your hiring process. As I've told many leaders, "You may not have an engagement issue – it could be a hiring issue."

It's often worthwhile to identify these highly engaged individuals at the outset of any attempts to improve engagement. They are your allies! As invested individuals, they already have an interest in seeing you succeed, and – importantly – they'd likely be happier at work if everyone were as committed as they are. If they are excellent communicators, that's even better! Seek out ways to make them ambassadors of your message, regardless of where they fall in the corporate hierarchy.

As another early move, be sure to establish that engagement is not about employee satisfaction. Neither is it about avoiding tough decisions. As you're rolling out your goals, whether they are directly related to engagement or not, the message is not, "What can the company do for you?" It's "Here's our collective goal, and here's how we'll get there together." If you cover this ground early on, you'll be in a better position to deal with the inevitable skeptics.

It's worth noting that a successful engagement strategy has the potential to turn skeptics into supporters. Having one's expectations surpassed is a powerful conversion experience. Don't ignore the unconvinced in your audience; let the clarity and consistency of your message overwhelm their doubts. If you manage even grudging acknowledgement of what you've accomplished, you are on your way to finding more productive uses for the energy and critical thinking skills that skeptics may have brought to bear in analyzing your attempts at engagement.

At ENSR, we knew we'd achieved a true change in the way our brand was perceived when Employee Engagement became the first subject to be discussed during operational review meetings. Previously, "soft" items like Human Resources related items, were relegated to the end of the agenda. This change was more than symbolic – it spoke louder than words.

TOOLS + PROCESSES

Construct a Communications "Waterfall"

If you wish to create engagement, you have to ensure that communication of all sorts is happening at all levels. Eventually, you want this to happen as effortlessly as a cascade pouring towards its destination. In reality, it will take some initial effort… and ongoing vigilance.

- *Identify your communications ambassadors.* Regardless of their communications talents, your initial recruits are those with management responsibility. Tell these people that their duties include transmitting the company's messages. Let them know that their performance in this arena will be evaluated… and follow up on that promise.

  If you have enthusiastic, engaged employees that are potential allies, enlist them too. Provide a forum for their input and give them well-defined communications tasks within their peer groups (and beyond, if appropriate).

- *Supply them with direct channels and appropriate tools.* Every important message from the top should be accompanied, at minimum, by general talking points for managers at all levels, an (anticipated) FAQ, and a means by which unanticipated questions are answered and publicized.

  Scale your tools to fit the task at hand! If a large-scale announcement or rollout needs to be communicated, look closely at the available vehicles and explore new options if they prove in any way limited or outdated. Engage your communications ambassadors in finding the most appropriate methods for your staff and its subgroups. And don't overlook the need to customize your communication approach depending on the audience. Although this point will be discussed in greater detail in Step 5, your Gen Y staff require a very different communication approach than your Boomers.

- *Monitor their progress.* After tasking managers and leaders with the responsibility to communicate, track how they're doing. Survey direct reports about how well messages have been communicated. Ask for paraphrases of each message, both from managers and their staff, to assess effectiveness in information transfer.

Publicize Your Strategic Plan

If you are communicating profit or revenue goals and milestones, you should also be communicating engagement goals and milestones. According to Aberdeen Group's research, having a formal engagement strategy is one of the key differentiators for "Best-in-Class" organizations. In fact, organizations with a formal engagement strategy are 83% more likely to be best-in-class than organizations with ad hoc engagement efforts[18].

Use whatever vehicles are handy, including those that might appear to be static (email, newsletters, the company intranet, letters from executives, etc.), as well as dynamic (Town Hall meetings, interactive department meetings, leadership workshops, and informal lunches). Do not underestimate the impact of "leadership by walking around" to help cascade your messaging. Make milestones clear, and define what will constitute success or failure along the way. If a shift in goals is necessary, communicate this as well. Don't apologize for the shift, just make the reasons for it well-known and the revised goalposts apparent.

Employees want to hear good news, but they also want transparency about bad news (or just about changes of direction that may affect them). Remember, this is the era of speed. As Thomas Friedman highlights in *The World is Flat*, technology and globalization have changed both the rules and the pace of change[19]. Organizations

---

18   *Beyond Satisfaction: Engaging Employees To Retain Customers*, Aberdeen Group report, July 2009

19   Friedman, Thomas L., The World is Flat: A Brief History of the 21st Century. New York, NY: Farrar, Straus and Giroux, 2005

that are not nimble and can't quickly adapt to change will be left behind.

Engagement will be impossible to quantify if it is not part of your strategic plan. While constructing your strategic plan, build in ways to measure engagement. Collect, collate, and communicate staff feedback. At each reporting juncture, ask yourself: "Are we seeing progress? If not, why not?" Communicate and celebrate your successes.

> **If you do not have an accurate means by which to align staff development goals with your training budget and its outcomes, put one in place. Monitor it monthly and compare expenditures to turnover. And figure out how to get "training" out of the cost column of your balance sheet. It is an investment, and your managers shouldn't use savings in training to pad profits.**

Set and Communicate Measurable Objectives

Sit down with your leadership team and define measurable things that you can assess and communicate. If you are interested in measuring engagement, determine your benchmarks and specific items to measure. Critical engagement metrics might include not only your percentage of voluntary turnover, but also what portion of that turnover is comprised of your top-rated employees (those who will likely also have been your most engaged). What are their stated reasons for leaving?

Training is another key engagement metric. How is your training budget being used? This is within the scope of responsibility of most managers, from the lowest ranks to the highest. Establish a means to track the progress of, and investment in, the highest- and lowest-performing employees.

Another metric that reflects engagement is employee referral percentages. Based on research by Aberdeen Group, top-performing companies (the top 20%) averaged a 19% year-over-year increase in employee referrals, while average-performing companies (the middle 50%) reported an average increase of only 10%. The bottom 30% of performing companies actually saw a 6% *decrease* in employee referrals[20].

---

[20] *Beyond Satisfaction: Engaging Employees To Retain Customers*, Aberdeen Group report, July 2009

You should be capturing data on what percent of new hires join your firm via employee referrals. If this figure is low, it indicates low engagement on the part of your existing staff. If you're showing positive trends, you're on your way to increasing engagement. Given the strong link between engaged employees and innovation, you should also determine how best to measure the creativity output of your employees. Are you measuring the quality and quantity of employees' ideas and suggestions? Are you tracking R+D trends by department? By business unit?

Establish Communication "Fountains"

Earlier, I used the metaphor of a water-fall to reinforce the need for cascading communication. Communication fountains – vehicles to propel communication upward – are also necessary for engagement to take hold. Employees must feel comfortable about communicating upward (more on specific mechanisms for this in Step 7). If individuals are afraid of approaching their "bosses" with questions or concerns, or if they sense that significant questions and concerns are not being followed up at the appropriate level, the company brand will suffer internally from a perception that what individuals think doesn't matter. This is a recipe for apathy – employees will balance the scale with minimal input and effort. Managers should:

- *Encourage questions* — Managers at all levels must be made aware that it is their responsibility to (a) answer according to the overarching message or (b) if the answer is beyond their knowledge of the subject, to push it to the upper echelon while assuring the questioner that an answer is forthcoming. (Of course, it's important to deliver on this promise. The responsibility lies with the manager who has posed the question to his or her superiors.)

- *Solicit feedback* — Whether it is positive or negative, managers must be provided a means by which to funnel input to the people responsible for processing and, if warranted, incorporating it. Employee engagement studies, conducted yearly, or preferably, biannually (with a pulse survey in the alternative years) are one mechanism to ensure that this happens. Communicating those results back is the way to complete the loop.

- *Share results* — Close the loop. Whether you use the above survey method or any other, it is critical to share results with the participants/vested individuals and to allow them to react. As with every other message, results (and corporate responses) must be cascaded from the top to the bottom of an organization.

Establish an Employee Engagement Committee

If engagement itself is among the objectives to be communicated, it is helpful to pool the resources in your organization who are most invested in seeing engagement take root and flourish.

An Employee Engagement Committee should consist of members of your Senior Leadership team and a cross sectional group of high-performing employees. The committee should be comprised of 10-20 people in total with "term limits" of two years (with half the team rotating every year to ensure continuity).

> **Cisco Systems assigned one of its most prestigious workforce councils to focus on engagement, and report progress directly to the CEO and his operating committee. This is a prime example of a visible and credible company commitment.**

A 50 -50 split between leaders and non-leaders is advisable. If 50% of your committee consists of members of your Senior Leadership Team, this will demonstrate upper-management commitment to the cause of employee engagement. Avoid allowing leaders to appoint non-management committee members. The ideal appointees are those who self-identify as being passionate about engagement, who are

enthused about being on the committee, and who don't view their appointment as "one more thing to do." (Of course, they have to receive the endorsement of their leader!)

The committee also needs teeth. It needs the authority to make decisions and enact them. A mixture of highly respected members of the leadership team will ensure that issues needing a rubber stamp are hastened onto the appropriate desk.

Make It Foolproof

As you are implementing any of the above processes, strive for simplicity at the programmatic level and precision in execution. There is often a tendency to come out of the gate overly ambitious and enthusiastic, and to commit to more than you can sustain or afford. Avoid initiative fatigue, or you risk running 90 yards in a 100-yard race. Under-promising and over delivering will protect against employee cynicism. ("They told us they would have this in place by May 1, and we've seen nothing!") It's often more important that a plan with some flaws be well-executed than that one that seems watertight be rolled out halfheartedly.

- *There has to be follow-up!* The institution of meaningful feedback loops is as important as, if not more important than, the tenets of the plan itself.

- *Commit to a few things.* Publicize your commitment to a handful of significant, measurable objectives. Then nail them, brand them, and communicate your success.

Use Available Technologies

Leverage your company's existing means of communication, or consider creating new ones that can support a variety of purposes. Use your PDA or email calendar to assist in follow up and to make sure you're doing the following items on a weekly basis:

- Recognize somebody.

- Communicate progress.

- Solicit feedback.

- Send your observations up the fountain.

More Of – Same-As – Less Of Feedback Sessions

One feedback tool I have found to be useful, flexible, and scalable is a facilitated session in which employees have an opportunity to provide feedback to a supervisor. The end result is a team's wish list for their leader: "What should (name) be doing more of?" "What should stay the same?" "What should there be less of?" In very simple terms, irrespective of topic, such a feedback process provides a direct means for input on any given program, process, department, or individual.

Guidelines for "More of/Same as/Less of" Feedback Exercise

PREP:

1. Agree on date/time/location. Try for an intimate setting (as opposed to a large conference room) unless size of group dictates a large space.

2. Make sure flipcharts (or large pieces of paper), markers, and tape are available.

3. Be aware of the context of the exercise, whether it is the middle of a staff meeting, or connecting people by phone. Remember to remain conscientious about everyone's ability to participate.

AT MEETING

1. Have manager set stage by explaining the purpose in his/her words.

2. Agree on a method of contacting the manager at the conclusion of the exercise.

3. After the manager leaves, elaborate on the purpose if necessary, and explain your role simply as "neutral facilitator." You will neither contribute nor comment on the content of their product. You are there to guide the process.

4. Set tone. This is a supportive session. It's a learning opportunity for participants as well (learning to give constructive feedback, learning how to reach consensus and understanding others' perspectives).

5. Ask about individual time constraints that may need to be considered or accommodated. (Typically I've found that even if people say they can only stay an hour, if the discussion is fruitful, they will stay for the length of the exercise - so don't worry about individual schedules setting the pace).

6. Start with a warm-up exercise by splitting the group in half (or in quarters). One group creates a list of "positive leadership traits," the other "negative leadership traits." Give five minutes for each group to create lists. Even if they're not finished at the time limit, cut the exercise off so you can focus the remaining energy on the main exercise. Bounce back and forth between the groups to stimulate free flow of ideas, encourage the scribe to record everything, even if it seems to be redundant. Don't let them get hung up on word use or spelling. Neither counts. Just quantity and "free flow."

7. At the conclusion of five minutes, have scribe hand marker to a person they select to be the presenter. Have each presenter "flesh out bullets" on flipchart.

8. Explain that this is a generic exercise to prime the pump for the real exercise - encourage the same level of free thinking and discussion.

MORE OF/SAME AS/LESS OF EXERCISE

1. Refocus the group with explanation of the three lists and how traits can often appear on two or three lists simultaneously (because of different circumstances).

2. Two rules: The group can only document traits that are consensus decisions, which diffuses the threat of one loud outlier. Secondly, what gets discussed in the room, stays in the room.

3. Assign scribes for each of the three lists (or one person can do all three).

4. Start with "same as" traits to get discussion flowing. Then let ideas spill into other flipcharts as they occur. You may need to facilitate this process at first — helping them recognize on which chart their idea should be recorded.

5. Try to take a back seat to discussion. Intervene if the group gets hung up on semantics, can't reach consensus, or are in need of ideas or words to express thoughts. Throw out some paraphrases or suggestions that they can consider.

6. Record lists in a notebook as they are created. Your copy of the lists will be given to the manager after the session.

7. Make sure the lists represent some balance and that double-edged comments show up on both "more of" *and* "less of" lists.

8. Encourage the group to find ways to express their ideas with humor or metaphors, especially on the "less of" list (e.g. "coffee" to convey hyperactivity or irritability, etc.)

9. As ideas wind down, refer back to "positive" and "negative" traits lists to ensure that all areas are covered. Check to make sure nobody is withholding comments (typically visible in body language).

10. Ask for volunteers to be "coaches" for each list. Remind them you will be there to help, and that it's a great learning experience.

11. After you select the coaches, provide them with the following guidelines:

    a) They are speaking for the group. They should use phrases like "We felt... We thought... The group agreed..."

    b) Solicit help from group for specific examples to clarify points.

    c) Provide as much detail as possible, so that the manager can fully grasp the group's meaning,

12. Remind non-coaches that they are to pipe in often and lend support.

13. Check the group's anxiety level. If necessary reassure them about the "ground rules" and their anonymity.

14. Contact the manager.

15. While the manager is in transit, take down all lists except the "Same As" list.

16. When the manager arrives, restate the ground rules:

    a) Consensus opinions only.

    b) The manager will be listening to accept, even though s/he may not necessarily agree.

    c) The manager will not be defending, but is encouraged to stop and ask questions to make sure s/he understands.

17. To assure the manager that no note-taking is necessary on his or her part, tell them that you have already recorded the three lists on a separate piece of paper that you will provide to him/her at the end of the session.

18. Have the coaches present all three lists. Try to keep silent and let the group do the work.

19. At the conclusion, thank the participants for their candor, and remind them that it is their job going forward to support the manager in his/her pursuit of enhanced leadership style. They are now "all in this together;" they should be the constant reminders and cheerleaders as time goes on.

20. Remember to give the manager copies of your handwritten duplicates of the lists.

To strengthen workforce diversity, we must create a culture of inclusion, cross-cultural understanding and collaboration.

– CHARLES R. LEE
Former Board Chairman,
Verizon Communications

STEP FIVE
INDIVIDUALIZE YOUR ENGAGEMENT

Early in my career, when I was beginning to view engagement as a key strategic pillar of business, I started with what seemed to me to be a logical question: "What does the company need to do to engage its employees?" I was looking for a one-size-fits-all approach, but I quickly learned that there isn't one. Everyone has their own inherent strengths and unique drivers that motivate them to excel in the workplace: things that may be based on their age, cultural background, gender, or tenure – or simply upon the skills they are most satisfied with exercising.

It may come as a surprise that money is not widely believed to be an engagement driver. From my experience, I've concluded that the vast majority of employees are motivated by achievement, and will behave according to how they are being measured (after all, who doesn't want to win). Money may be a logical way to recognize superior efforts, and its use as a measurement might drive motivation. But it is the measurement, and not the money, that is the driver. Daniel Pink's best-selling book *Drive* provides some excellent observations and studies that reinforce this premise. Pink reinforces the notion that one's intrinsic motivational drivers almost always trump external motivational drivers like money[21].

Workforce Trends: Engagement and the Different Generations

Perhaps more than ever before, it is common to find a workforce that is composed of people of a wide variety of ages, with interests that depend to a large extent on their upbringing, their current goals, and their future plans. Although the categories below are generalizations (and more applicable for the Western world), most readers will recognize truth in the traits associated with generational differences on the job.

Traditionalists – Born between 1922 and 1945, Traditionalist workers are motivated by conformity, stability, security, and upward mobility. They tend to view loyalty to their country as an imperative (1a), but with loyalty to their company a strong second (1b). The statement "I will give my all to my company" resonates with Traditionalists with nearly the same intensity as "I will fight for my country." They take pride in doing their work consistently, dependably, and well, but are not particularly motivated by the latest technological tools or the "hottest" trends in management. A respect for authority also characterizes this generation, and their fidelity to the company often blends seamlessly with their loyalty to superiors and coworkers.

21 Pink, Daniel H. Drive: The Surprising Truth about What Motivates Us. New York, NY: Riverhead Hardcover 2009

With impending retirement, Traditionalists are often motivated by the desire to leave the workforce in security and comfort, and pleased that they fulfilled their employment obligations to their company. Along with the Boomer generation, however, in tight economic times they may postpone retirement until their retirement savings recover, which can lead to tensions among younger staff looking to move up the ladder.

Boomers – Generally identified as being born between the years of 1946 and 1964, Boomers are idealistic, finding personal and social expression deeply important. The first generation to earn and possess more than their parents, they also tend to be ambitious, materialistic, and prone to workaholism.

Boomers enjoy opportunities for expression, and are among the ranks of workers who are truly engaged by meetings – especially when ideas that intrigue them are being exchanged. They also remember when getting email was a good thing, and not overwhelming.

Questioning authority, a tenet for masses of young people in the 1960s and 70s, is still very much a part of the Boomer approach to life and to work. They are far more apt to challenge leadership than Traditionalists, and also somewhat more prone to embrace change. Although Boomers are highly achievement-oriented and driven to vie for more money and greater responsibility, another key engagement driver for this generation is their love of collaboration. The idealism that encouraged many of this generation to boycott the Vietnam War still kindles a desire to be part of "something bigger," and they tend to be highly engaged by working in partnership or as part of a team.

Following the model established above, Boomers tend to be loyal to their careers (1a), and their company (1b).

Generation X – The first generation to insist on work/life balance, this group, born between 1965 and 1980, also includes more women (as well as men who have assumed more home and family responsibilities). In contrast to Boomers, an excess

of work will not engage Gen X – in fact, it is apt to provoke the response that "life isn't just material." Independence and free agency are watchwords for Gen X, and they may become cynical with regards to their jobs if they sense that these things are not honored.

Gen X is the first generation to grow up with technology and, in terms of communication, often prefer email (or electronic bulletins or newsletters) to attending meetings.

In addition, flexibility is very important for this group, and despite the perception by some of their older peers that they work less, they usually make up for the time they've taken to attend a child's play or soccer game by working nights or weekends. In fact, Gen X is currently quite career-oriented, seeing themselves as next in line to take the reins. As older workers stay on in the workplace to boost their retirement, or simply because they "love to work," Gen X can grow impatient. Their continued engagement depends on the sense that, in their place of work, they are learning and growing. Training and development are consequently huge engagement drivers for this group, as are mentoring opportunities.

Caught between Boomers and Gen Y, there is growing unrest among Gen X workers. Deloittes' 2009 Human Capital study reports that only 37% of Gen X plan to remain with their employer for the next 12 months[22].

Gen X employees' work loyalties seem to lie first with their careers (1a) and then with their immediate supervisors (1b). They may well be content, or even eager, to follow a boss or supervisor to the next career stop.

---

[22]   *Managing talent in a turbulent economy*, Special Report on Talent Retention: Deloitte, September 2009

> Where Gen X workers might prefer mid-year performance feedback in addition to their annual performance review, Gen Y is more prone to ask "How am I doing today?"

Generation Y – Born between 1981 and 2000, this digitally oriented group is characterized by hope about the future; social activism; family-centricity; and the desire for diversity. Having grown up well after the advent of computers and mobile phones, Gen Y is accustomed to instant communication and information at their fingertips. Increasingly, they ignore both phones and email in favor of text messaging: a trend that a company whose communication policy involves lengthy missives from the CEO would do well to recognize.

Predictably, they are also highly drawn to new technologies, especially those which grant them increased mobility and flexibility in their jobs. The latest, smallest, and most portable technology is far more likely to engage a Gen Y employee than a cumbersome desktop tower.

Before the recession of 2008-2009, the average tenure for Gen Y was a mere 20 months, making issues such as job location and the ability to evolve within a company important engagement factors. Gen Y can be motivated to stay with a firm if allowed the challenge and novelty of doing different jobs, or doing the same jobs differently. Unlike Traditionalists or, to a lesser extent, even Boomers and Gen X employees, Gen Y is not particularly concerned with permanence or security. Many view abruptly changing career directions or moving back in with parents to be perfectly acceptable solutions if they are dissatisfied with their situations. Workforce experts speculate that the memories of today's recession will be short-lived, and that Gen Y will quickly revert to their pre-recession frequency of job changes.

Although it's early to assert trends for this generation, it seems that Gen Y's loyalties rank with themselves (as 1a), and with their families and social networks (as 1b).

While Boomers might happily go years between performance appraisals, recognition, praise, and constructive criticism are not only welcomed by Generation Y (and to a lesser extent, Generation X), but active means to motivate them. Receiving a continuous flow of positive feedback is an important engagement driver. This was the generation that was somewhat pampered by Boomer parents: the classic example being sports trophies for both winning and losing teams, and traditional A, B, C, D, F school grades replaced by less stratified systems (Exceeding/Meeting/Below Expectations, for example).

Some Points of Connection

Generalizations, of course, can only get you so far. But knowing the traits that members of a particular generation have in common can help to start the vital conversation that gets at what drives an individual. One particular Gen X woman I supervised was incredibly driven by recognition – money was practically irrelevant to her. I made sure that she had plenty of face time with executives whenever the opportunity arose. Conversely, a Boomer in his late 50s, whom I also supervised, showed signs of becoming disengaged during a period when layoffs were necessary. Recognizing that security – a key driver for him – was at risk, I frequently went out of my way to reassure him that his job was in no danger.

Despite their differences, all generations share the need for fairness and the desire to achieve. These are the values that underwrite engagement across the board. Intriguingly, too, the frisson between different generations' drivers can influence the engagement of the company as a whole. One emergent trend of this sort is Boomers' increasing interest in corporate social responsibility, an issue that Gen Y is primarily responsible for bringing to the culture. Gen Y wants to work for a "company that cares" – one that donates to charities, is concerned with reducing its carbon footprint or other environmental impacts, and embraces volunteerism.

Working alongside this younger generation seems to be inspiring Boomers to the levels of activism they may associate with their youth. After having climbed the corporate ladder and accumulated the things their parents could not afford, some demographic experts are predicting that there will be a resurgence of concern

about social and environmental issues. (See Step 6 for more on corporate social responsibility as a motivating factor.)

This trend reinforces my belief (which I'll discuss at more length shortly) that diversity in the workplace, be it generational, social, or cultural, is precisely the kind of soil that fosters innovation… And innovation is, ultimately, what a company needs in order to survive.

Engagement and Globalization

In the United States and other parts of the Western world, Gen Y is projected to be the first generation that will not make as much money as their parents. But in developing nations, this is not the case. Gen Y workers in third-world nations share a lot of characteristics with Boomers. As with the latter group in the West, an Indian or Chinese employee in his or her 20s may be seeing opportunities that their parents were never offered. So, while the rapid spread of industrialization and technology is blurring the geographic (and some cultural) boundaries, global companies need to be aware that engagement drivers are very different in, say, Beijing than in Melbourne, and that their strategy must change accordingly. The desire for work/life balance that is so pronounced among younger generations in the United States is, for the most part, not shared by their Chinese counterparts – in fact, offering policies to promote the U.S. standard would likely backfire. Again, like their Boomer counterparts in the West, most Gen X and Gen Y Asians work long hours, and like Traditionalists, they are nearly as committed to their companies as they are to their families.

Authors Daniel Pink (*A Whole New Mind*[23]) and Thomas Friedman (*The World is Flat*[24]) have recently garnered deserved attention for their interpretations of this phenomenon. (Pink uses the phrase "Abundance, Asia, and Automation" to describe the impending future of business.) Observable facts are rendering the ascendance of Asia far more than a mere trend; I can think of no better example to illustrate the importance of individualizing engagement.

---

[23] Pink, Daniel H. A Whole New Mind: Moving from the Information Age to the Conceptual Age. New York, NY: Riverhead Hardcover, 2005

[24] Friedman, Thomas L., The World is Flat: A Brief History of the 21st Century, New York, NY: Farrar, Straus and Giroux, 2005

Engagement, Diversity, and Inclusion

For much of my early career, diversity in the workplace was primarily driven by compliance. Laws to guarantee equal opportunity regardless of age, gender, race, and physical ability had many companies scrambling to prove (and to protect) themselves. In some progressive cities like San Francisco, protections for sexual orientation were already taking root. Although clearly there remains much work to be done in this arena and vigilance is still required, in many ways the term "diversity" is being replaced by "inclusion," and becoming a more seamless and organic part of the way we do business. As Friedman points out in *The World is Flat*, technology is the great leveler. In both our business and personal lives, it's technology that connects us with people across the globe. (My son takes for granted that his video game teammates and opponents hail from China and India as well as his native North America.)

John Dionisio, president and CEO of AECOM Technology Corporation, has demonstrated his understanding of the need for generational diversity by inviting junior "up-and-comers" to the annual Planning Council Meeting – a significant strategic session previously reserved for top-level executives. The benefit? Senior-level employees get valuable information from their more junior colleagues, and these junior colleagues are further engaged by their participation in discussions about where this large architectural and engineering company is headed.

Marilyn Nagle, Chief Diversity Officer at Cisco Systems, believes companies have an opportunity to leverage technology to booster their inclusion and diversity efforts. "At Cisco, our inclusion and diversity business drivers are globalization, collaboration, and innovation. Technology (webinars, social networks, video pods, etc.) allows us to economically bring together diverse teams from across the globe that reinforce these three important drivers." Nagle claims that Cisco's inclusion and diversity momentum reached historic heights after CEO John Chambers hosted a global Inclusion and Diversity Symposium utilizing a virtual webinar, underwriting the idea that technology can be an ally in diversity efforts.

> It's not always smooth sailing. I'm sure many travelling executives have similar faux pas under their belts, but I remember being quite embarrassed once after giving a female colleague in Malaysia a hug. (I'd just come from Brazil, where such a thing wouldn't cause anyone to bat an eye.) Although I'd known my Malaysian colleague for years, due to cultural differences, a male-female embrace was inappropriate in the workplace.

Smart companies understand that diversity is both broader and more subtle than compliance laws, however necessary, can cover. "Diversity," for many companies, is an end in and of itself. "Inclusion," on the other hand, means that the end is a better product or result. I am an enthusiastic advocate for as much inclusion (whether by generation, skillset, tenure, or culture) as possible on any given task team or project. Not only do these enriched groups come up with more comprehensive solutions, you will have broader support for a solution if different constituencies within your company feel they've had a voice.

Global employers need to keep up to speed with the transition toward "inclusion," and to begin to digest and incorporate cultural differences (especially as they affect communication) not as a program, but as a simple matter of doing business. Do the heads of your teams and divisions look like your company? Does your company look like your clients?

In the graphic on the following page, the inner ring tends to represent the traditional "diversity" focuses with which most businesses are already quite familiar (often driven by compliance). The outer ring represents some considerations that are often overlooked, but that are the unseen contributors to an individual's motivation and behavior on the job. I don't recommend that the significance of the inner wheel be disregarded, but I do suggest that to create a successful, inclusive culture, these considerations need to be broadened to include the outer ring. In assembling a task or project team, "inclusion" may mean bringing together people who fall into differently-defined categories than many companies have been accustomed to use.

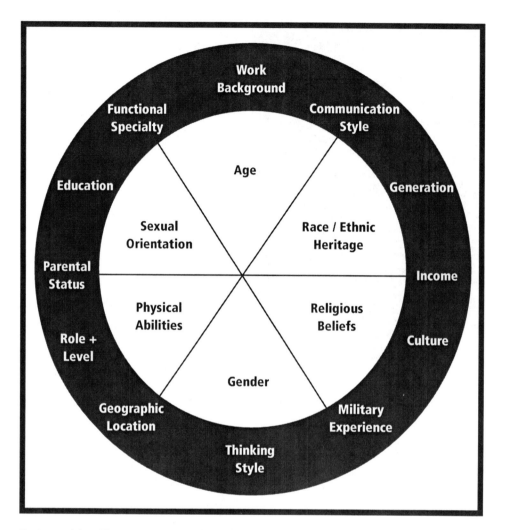

Perhaps it's glib to point out that this is the future of business, and that the companies that focus on inclusion will have a distinct advantage. But there is an obscure quote, the source of which I've never been able to find, that's always inspired me: "Don't ask the architect of the present to design your future." Now, as never before, we can leverage diversity of all kinds to make sure that our future has the broadest foundation… and the highest potential.

Engagement and Tenure

It makes sense that engagement levels are highest for new hires. After all, they're entering the job full of hope and enthusiasm… which may quickly fall off if they become disengaged. Studies by Wright Associates show that it takes an average of

> In an effort to boost inclusion, many companies will leverage the leadership talent brought in via a merger or acquisition. AECOM, for example, has used their M+A platform to expand and diversify their leadership, thereby creating an influx of new ideas and visions. This has further enhanced staff engagement by contributing to employees' perception that even the newest opinions are being heard.

seven years for levels of engagement to return to their initial "year one" peak, with turnover highest between years two and six. What is your organization doing to re-energize that two-to-six year employee?

Many companies boast that they have a lot of long-termers, and view long tenure as a sign of engagement. But especially in a down economy, it is important to make sure that those people have not plateaued – otherwise, you may be looking at an exodus when other opportunities present themselves to your staff. Worse, you may be providing job security for a group of complacent, satisfied, and perhaps underperforming employees. Job tenure should be an outcome and not a goal of your engagement initiatives.

"Stay" Interviews"

Your company likely conducts exit interviews, but talking to employees once they've made the decision to leave is of limited use in retention. You need to re-recruit the staff that you have by asking why they are staying, and by finding out how to further engage them. Why not conduct "stay" interviews? Periodically asking your employees the questions highlighted on the next page might help uncover and rectify some disengagement drivers at a critical early juncture.

Identify and Brand Your Engagement Differentiators

Why do people work for your company? Every workplace has some engagement merit, or it would be out of business. Lisa Zankman, Senior Vice President of Human Resources at Beth Israel Deaconess Medical Center, says, "We interview people with the goal of identifying candidates who are committed to taking care of people,' thereby reinforcing the hospital's culture. In addition, hospital CEO Paul Levy leverages new communications technologies to the hilt: he blogs, he Tweets, and he is on Facebook. (Not surprisingly, Zankman says he is "extremely popular

KEY "STAY INTERVIEW" QUESTIONS

- **How can the company help you be more successful in your job?**

- **Are we allowing you to reach your maximum potential?**

- **What would make you leave (our company) for another job?**

- **If there are three things we can change around here that would help you and others realize your potential, what would they be?**

with everyone, but especially our younger employees.")

You need to learn the top three or four things that differentiate you from your competitors. Companies tend to do this on the marketing side (Why do customers choose us?) but not on the internal side (Why do people want to work here?).

Conduct "stay" interviews with the top 100 performers at your firm, and you will learn about a common set of drivers that should become your differentiators. Then leverage them. Do more of them. And brand and market them internally! Everyone wants to be proud of where they work. Give them a reason to get excited about your brand. At ENSR, engagement was one of our differentiators. We consistently communicated that we cared deeply about our employees – wanted to cultivate them, communicate to them, and grow with them. When they promoted me – the "people guy" – to COO, some of our technical staff were boasting about it to clients as proof of our engagement culture! (I should also point out that we also communicated regularly with our employees about the mutual commitment to high performance. We cared about our employees, but we needed our employees, reciprocally, to care deeply about the financial health of the business).

One of the challenges in a job with extremely high career security (as with a union, government group, or academic position) is that engagement differentiators are harder to distinguish from simple benefits. This is why it is important to interview the employees who, despite the obvious perks available to everyone, are your top performers. What drives these people to go above and beyond? These are the values that you need to be selling internally.

Define Your Engagement Objectives

In concert with determining what distinguishes you from your competition in terms of engagement, you must set concrete objectives to promote your organization's larger goals. What are you trying to accomplish? If you want to hire the best, an objective should be to retain your best employees in order to cultivate an environment where the best want to work. The perception of a great place to work will get more applicants. Maybe the goal is client satisfaction – what does that mean? Your objective might be to hire engaged employees who have the traits and behaviors that your clients value, or it might be to put existing employees with those traits and behaviors in client stewardship or liaison positions. If you learn from employee surveys that your company's hiring and retention is being negatively impacted by the perception that you lack corporate responsibility, how do you change that opinion? Your objectives might include donating monies to particular causes, or volunteering for charity events, or cutting off purchases from manufacturers in countries that have unfair labor laws.

If you think employee engagement is important, what are your objectives? You need to discern the ones that work best for the individuals who comprise your company.

From the Trenches...

In support of our engagement efforts at ENSR, I wanted a corporate university – a highly visible means to cultivate and train our staff, and to encourage the exchange of ideas (See Step 6 for more on this). There was little to no budget to create a whole suite of new development programs, but I knew we had to start somewhere – so we created ENSR University, and started by promoting the training that we already had. Every week, some communication was distributed under the ENSR University brand about the opportunities that were already available and about how staff were making use of them. No more dollars were being spent, but the perception that ENSR was invested in cultivating its staff for success took hold and grew, and engagement scores went off the charts. Once we did have the money to fund additional training programs, we made sure to publicize them thoroughly as well – fortifying employees' trust in our commitment. I have come to be a big champion of internal promotion. All companies have something good to offer – determining what those things are, and then communicating the hell out of them, will give you more traction than you can imagine.

TOOLS + PROCESSES

Employee Development Plan (EDP)

One of the more extensive occasions that supervisors have to discuss what drives an individual to put in discretionary effort is the performance appraisal – however, as discussed in Step 4, these conversations often focus too thoroughly on what an employee does at the expense of why. At ENSR, we chose to shift from performance appraisals to individualized Employee Development Plans (EDPs), tailored to identify engagement drivers. These plans occasioned dialogue between staff and management about what was working, what wasn't, and how engagement might be deepened.

The stated purpose of the EDP was "to motivate and guide… employees to perform at the highest levels, and to focus on the employee's professional growth." We took care to point out that the plan was not to be viewed just as a "report card," but rather as a roadmap for continuous development. Because the completed plan often included 360-degree feedback as well as input from both the employee and the manager, it overcame or went above the limitations of a typical performance review, and thus was far richer.

Managers were instructed to spend as much (or more) time discussing future goals as on reviewing performance. In addition to explicitly linking the employee's goals to the company's strategic priorities, the plan sought input on longer-term career interests and ways to enhance overall engagement. The result was an open, yet formal, discussion not only of accomplishments or shortfalls, but also of the factors (passions, training and development, family situation, immediate and long-term career goals) that the manager and the company should take into consideration in cultivating the particular individual's excellence.

Recent research validates the business benefit for managers and employees to jointly develop and agree on performance goals. A recent Aberdeen Group survey reported that 90% of their "Best-in-Class" companies, defined as the top 20% in overall performance, have their managers and employees agree on performance goals[25].

---

[25] *Beyond Satisfaction: Engaging Employees to Retain Customers.* Aberdeen Group report, July 2009

In response to the needs of our Gen X and Y staff (discussed earlier), we also introduced formal mid-year "checkups" that allowed for an additional sit-down meeting to review goals, developmental areas, and accomplishments. This customization, based on what we knew and learned about the individuals who comprised our staff, typified the kind of individualization that ultimately boosted engagement – and drove the expenditure of discretionary effort – at our firm. This practice is further validated by Aberdeen's research, in which 83% of "Best-in-Class" companies' managers and employees hold regular, informal feedback sessions.

SAMPLE EMPLOYEE DEVELOPMENT PLAN (EDP)

Employee Name: _____

Review Period: From _____ **to** _____

Position Title: _____

Office/Department: _____

Salary Grade: _____

Supervisor Name: _____

Instructions:
The purpose of the EDP is to motivate and guide our employees to perform at the highest levels, and to focus on the employee's professional growth. Special emphasis should be placed on 1) aligning employee goals with Company strategy, goals, and values, and 2) the employee's professional and career development goals.

(Continued on following page)

A	B	C	D
Manager Completes Employee Development Plan Form	**Manager Reviews Draft Plan with Second-Level Manager**	**Manager + Employee Discuss Feedback + Agree on Goals for Upcoming Year**	**Manager + Employee Sign Form + Submit to HR Manager**
Manager completes Section 1, including: 1. A summary of performance, indicating progress made against goals set in the last EDP. 2. A feedback summary, commenting on the employee's strengths and improvement areas. It's recommended that managers get input from clients, peers, and others using a 360-degree Performance Feedback Form. The employee should also complete the EDP form as a self-assessment, and submit to the manager prior to meeting.	Manager and second-level manager meet to review performance feedback and discuss priority goals for employee before manager meets with the employee. Manager should partner with their HR Manager as needed for guidance on writing effective goals, providing reinforcing and constructive feedback, etc.	Manager and employee discuss results and accomplishments against goals, and feedback about strengths and improvement areas. Both clarify and agree on performance and development goals for the upcoming year and record in Section 2. Spend as much, or more, time discussing future goals as is spent on "reflecting" on past performance results.	After meeting, both the manager and employee sign this form, retaining copies for their files. Then, the manager submits to the Human Resources Manager.

1. GOAL ACCOMPLISHMENT+FEEDBACK ON SKILLS + COMPETENCIES

WHAT Was Accomplished. Comment here on progress achieving professional and career development goals. Indicate development actions taken, including internal and external training, degree, certificate programs, professional registrations or certifications, etc.

HOW Results Were Achieved. Describe the employee's strengths and improvement areas. Be specific. Use 360-degree feedback and the employee's self-assessment and incorporate that feedback into your summary; do not include specific quotes or names.

Strengths:

Improvement Areas:

2. PERFORMANCE + DEVELOPMENT AGREEMENT

Performance Goals for Upcoming Year		
Goals/Measures:	Link to Strategic Plan	Timeframe for Completion

Professional Development Goals for Upcoming Year		
Choose 1-2 development goals to focus on this year to enhance performance in the current role. Review the key strengths and improvement areas from Section 1, and consider focusing on at least 1 strength to leverage and at least 1 improvement area. Include the specific actions that will be taken to achieve these goals;		
Goals / Focus Areas	Learning / Development Actions	Timeframe for Completion

(Continued on following page)

Professional Development Goals for Longer Term
(Within Three Years)

Identify 1-2 development goals to help make progress toward longer-term career interests. Comment on next possible jobs or stretch assignments that will help to develop for a longer-term, desired position. If you wish to continue in your current position longer term, identify ways to enhance your overall job satisfaction.

Goals / Focus Areas	Learning / Development Actions	Timeframe for Completion

Professional Development Goals for Longer Term
(Within Three Years)

Opportunities for temporary or permanent work around the world, provide both technical and personal learning that can enhance your career and develop a wide range of skills.

Are you willing to relocate if the opportunity arises? ☐ Yes ☐ No	Would you consider an extended assignment? ☐ Yes ☐ No

Employee Comments:

After meeting with your manager, you may add your comments here (attach additional sheets if necessary:

Signatures:

Our signatures indicate that we have seen, discussed, and understand the contents of this Employee Development Plan.

Employee: _____ **Date:** _____

Manager: _____ **Date:** _____

HR Manager: _____ **Date:** _____

Motivation is the art of getting people to do what you want them to do because they want to do it.

– DWIGHT D. EISENHOWER

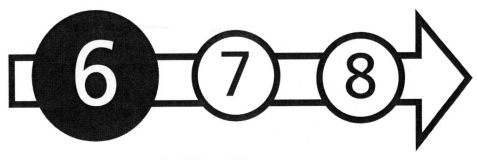

STEP SIX
CREATE A MOTIVATIONAL CULTURE

When I address an audience and tell them that in order to create an environment where staff can excel, there must be a commitment to and investment in training and development, one response in particular stands out to me. "I understand that it's important, but too many firms pour money into developing their staff only to have them leave for a competitor within a short while." While I understand this concern, I have to counter it with a question: "Would you prefer that you *don't* train and develop them, and then have them stay for 20 years?" I can think of no better way to ensure mediocrity, and few worse ones for employee engagement.

Now that much of the West's manufacturing is being outsourced to developing nations, we truly are living in an era where most companies' competitive advantage – the

> To better reflect the spectrum of growth opportunities, organizations should consider renaming – and rebranding – their "Training and Development" programs as "Learning" programs. Traditional classroom training, e-learning, attendance at conferences, external programs, mentoring, coaching, and stretch assignments should be included under this umbrella.

knowledge within the heads of their people – goes home at night. Just as a retail store must groom its assets by offering new or expanded products or a good-looking storefront, firms must also invest in their people.

Like so much else that characterizes engagement, training represents a trust-building reciprocal commitment: how can we as a company help you the employee, and how can you as an employee help us? Training and development opportunities are one of the surest paths to a mutually satisfying outcome. This is especially true as Boomers begin to retire and Gen X ascends. While Gen X may suffer from "middle child syndrome," the leaders of tomorrow will emerge from this generation, and how an organization deals with their development will surely influence that company's standing in the decades to come. Up-and-coming stars need mentorship and training. They need to be challenged with assignments that go above and beyond their job descriptions. They need "stretch" assignments that will test their succession potential.

In recessionary times, building a learning culture becomes more of a challenge because training dollars may need to be balanced against more immediate priorities such as cash flow, cost management, and "meeting plan" for this quarter. But the equation is quite simple: talent will grow at the companies that invest in it. Training and development is increasingly a key factor in the choice of where new talent applies for work. If you are known as a company that cultivates its employees, your brand is going to attract a wider pool of candidates than your more complacent competitors. Long term, this business model is simply more sustainable.

Part of your reputation-building should include instituting (and marketing) a culture of promotion from within – it can be disengaging if a company is always

e excellent example is Cisco Systems' "Vision to Strategy to Execution" chart, picted in a slightly simplified form on the following page. The chart serves as : template for their leaders to build line of sight within their businesses.

e Communication Commitment (discussed in Step 7) ensures that the employee participating in dialogue about where the company is headed and its strategic in to get there. Each then needs to share how they would like to grow, and cover how the company can support them in that goal. You want staff to be :ing, "Where is my career going? If I'm ambitious, how will I advance, and how he company investing in my future?" You want them confident in saying, "I ow the strategic plan, and I know where I fit in."

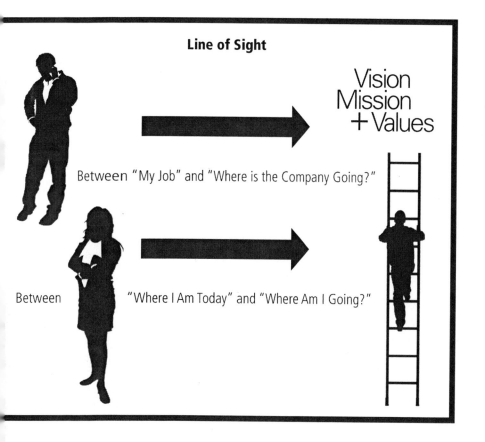

Line of Sight

Vision
Mission
+Values

Between "My Job" and "Where is the Company Going?"

Between   "Where I Am Today" and "Where Am I Going?"

hiring from the outside. There is a balance; successful firms als
workforce with new hires (and new ideas), while developing a stab
next-in-liners.

Leaders Have to Develop Themselves First

As companies evolve (in terms of globalization, technology,
acquisitions, growth, new markets, emerging competitors, etc.),
increasingly complex. I've had the pleasure of working closely with
(of Harvard Business School), when he was a member of ENSR's Board
He had a saying that I've often quoted: "Companies have to be car
'The Law of Getting Stupider and Stupider.'" Ben's warning is simple
is not increasing its own knowledge at the same pace as the size and
their company, they are effectively getting dumber by the day.

In much the way that, when being instructed on safety as an airli
you're told to put on your own oxygen mask before assisting your
theirs, leaders have to continue to develop themselves to keep pace v
while also developing their staff. If they do not, they will soon disco
skill set is now insufficient for a larger and more complex company
They also risk losing the respect of their staff if they're perceived as k
their heads." Leaders need to stay current, by which I mean learning
can about changes in their marketplace; emerging new technologie
the service or product offerings of their competitors; and the op
globalization. They also need to share their knowledge with staff
basis, and invite them to do the same.

Engaged Employees See a "Line of Sight" in their Careers

In Step 4, I stressed the engagement value of communicating yo
vision, values, and strategy to your staff, and referred to this nee
"line of sight." But in a sense, this is only laying the groundwork.
important for companies to create a line of sight between their stra
individual's job – and one might look at this as the macro level. I
equally important for companies to focus on the micro level as well
a clear picture of where individuals are today in their careers, and w
going.

	STRATEGY
VISION A global, engaged workforce united by one vision, one destiny that inspires us to be "Best in the World, Best for the World."	• **Power of the Generations:** Ensure relevance to the evolving needs of the four generations in the global workplace. • **Future of Work:** Unleash new working models that leverage collaboration + technology. • **Career Acceleration:** Invite people to come for the opportunity + stay for the lifetime experience. • **Inclusiviity:** A culture that values inclusion + diversity in all business aspects.
	Bring assets together to connect people strategies to the Business + Technology Architecture: • **The People:** Leadership, management, and team. • **The Culture:** Values + work experience. • **The Environment:** Employee workplace + services. • **The Opportunity:** Career opportunity + development. • **The Rewards:** Compensation + Recognition **EXECUTION**

Source: Cisco Systems, 2009

Relationship with Corporate Social Responsibility

With apologies to the Gordon Geckos of the world, seldom in the history of the Western world has greed been less popular. As I write this, government, society, customers, and employees are all looking with disdain upon corporate policies and practices that accrue wealth to an elite group while ignoring the issues that surround every one of us. Even if you are a business-to-business enterprise, these days your clients, vendors, stakeholders, and – especially – your employees are all demanding a higher level of responsibility. Your business integrity; carbon footprint; level of volunteerism; and efforts in giving back to your community are all being assessed.

One cannot read Thomas Friedman's *The World is Flat* without concluding that tomorrow's companies will need to have "the brains of a business school graduate and the heart of a social worker." There is increasing evidence that Baby Boomers and Generation Y workers (likely at opposing ends of the experience/engagement curve) share an interest in social responsibility. In addition to their paycheck and benefits, a large portion of your staff will want to see that the company they work for is making a difference in the world. With every passing day (and every headline), this becomes a more important engagement driver.

A significant corporate social responsibility initiative at the Timberland Company is its "Path of Service" policy, which provides all full-time employees with 40 hours of paid time off for community service annually (part timers receive 20 hours). Although there is a cost to the program (for example, when Timberland's retail stores occasionally operate with a reduced staff, to accommodate the commitment to community service), it is more than offset in other ways.

Upon joining Timberland in a senior operations role, John Pazzani suggested cutting this program for retail employees to help the company's performance in the tough retail economic climate of 1995. CEO Jeff Swartz said that he'd consider that suggestion, but only after Pazzani had "done his time" and participates in a Timberland-organized community service event. After his service experience (a day of cleaning up along walking / hiking trails) Pazzani returned with a dramatically revised perspective that has led him to become the company's Chief Culture Officer. "It may be a costly benefit," he says, "but we don't lose people." He's right: Timberland's voluntary turnover is in the mid single digits, a figure virtually unheard of in the retail business. In addition, there is an external communications benefit: when a Timberland store hangs up a sign indicating that staff are out on community service, customers frequently ask that they go one step further – providing a sign-up sheet whereby non-employees can participate!

Timberland CEO Swartz says that although people like to say crisis builds character, he believes it reveals character. He's right. Your employees are paying explicit attention to what you do when times are tough economically. That means that social responsibility can't be a "program" that gets cut when the bottom line is slipping. It must be embedded in the very essence of how your company is

run. If it is a "flavor of the month," employees will detect its transitory nature very quickly. As I've stressed throughout this book, actions speak louder than words. Implementing a policy of social responsibility means that you follow through – if you don't, the internal perception, and perhaps even the external perception, will be devastating.

In his book *Built to Last*, **Jim Collins delivers a succinct summation of the importance of corporate social responsibility: it provides purpose above and beyond profit** [26]. **"In a truly great company," Collins states, "profits and cash flow become like blood and water to a human body: they are absolutely essential for life, but they are not the point of life." Your employees likely sense this already – don't disregard it.**

To formalize commitment to communities in which its thousands of employees work and live, AECOM created the Community Trust, whereby approximately 2% of the company's profit goes to charitable efforts across the globe. These include local efforts like the adoption of a homeless shelter in the United Kingdom; pro-bono work for a Wilderness Trust in Africa; and local charity runs and rides in Australia to support natural disaster aid. In response to the 2010 Haiti earthquake, AECOM provided over $600k in relief effort donations (made possible by a combination of employee donations and company matches).

"To stay focused on business alone is no longer sustainable," Andrew Savitz writes in *The Triple Bottom Line*. "People want to work for responsible companies [27]." And increasingly, as discussed in Step 5, this desire is being expressed not only by Generation Y workers, but also by Baby Boomers as they are entering the "back nine" of their careers, with many hierarchical and monetary successes under their belts. "How do I give back?" these people are wondering. "How can I persuade my company to give back, too?" This cross-generational interest in a company's underlying social contributions is a powerful means of staff cohesion, as well as a key engagement driver: one that you cannot afford to neglect.

[26]   Collins, James C. and Porras, Jerry I. Built to Last: Successful Habits of Visionary Companies. New York, NY: HarperCollins, 1994

[27]   Savitz, Andrew W. with Weber, Karl. The Triple Bottom Line: How Today's Best-Run Companies Are Achieving Economic, Social and Environmental Success - and How You Can Too. San Francisco, CA: John Wiley and Sons, 2006

Often, your employees themselves can locate the volunteer programs or charitable giving that will fit into your budget. Their enthusiasm can work to your advantage as you find the top two or three ways to invest in corporate social responsibility – and as you publicize those investments both internally and externally.

Some social responsibility efforts are embedded in organizational metrics (again reiterating the connection between measurement and results). At Corning Glass, for instance, a set percentage of managers' "management by objectives" (MBO) criteria specifically addresses community service.

Other social responsibility efforts are entirely voluntary. I recently moderated a global webinar on the subject, and had the pleasure to meet with and introduce Jonathan Reckford, CEO of Habitat for Humanity: an organization dedicated to constructing housing for the poor that is primarily funded by charitable donations. Habitat for Humanity works with companies of all types and sizes, and although some have social responsibility budgets, the vast majority of initiatives are entirely driven by volunteer efforts. According to Jonathan, "The one consistent takeaway I hear from all company volunteers is that they receive more than they give when they work on one of our homebuilding projects."

During this webinar, a number of companies presented their best practices and current initiatives with regards to social responsibility – and although I shouldn't have been surprised, the engagement level of those presenting was off the charts!

Leverage Social Networks and Blogs

A common theme throughout this book is communication – the need to establish and maintain an ongoing exchange between employees, management, and the world outside the organization. In Step 5, I discussed the need to individualize engagement, and went into some detail about common engagement drivers that influence different generations of employees. There is one common thread in communication channels today that smart companies will not overlook: the proliferation of social networks utilized by many younger workers as their primary means of information exchange.

The trepidation that many organizations have about leveraging these channels is understandable. As access to information becomes more and more rapid and

uncomplicated, there are legitimate worries. Real-time communication has both benefits and drawbacks. Paul Levy, CEO of Beth Israel Deaconess Medical Center, smartly leverages social media. When he started his blog (runningahospital. blogspot.com, discussed in Step 7) in 2008 to better communicate with employees, most of his advisors told him not to do it. "What if you have to go back on something you've said?" they asked. "Is it wise to give our competitors access to this information?" Levy's response? "Any organization that is not leveraging social networks is missing an opportunity." While acknowledging the legitimacy of the concerns, he has managed to speak to a significant cross-section of his staff in a forum that they already take for granted – and to date, he has had great success.

John Chambers, President and CEO of Cisco Systems, communicates what's on his mind to all employees via a video blog every quarter. This communication is paired with "We Are Cisco," a tool which links all Cisco employees and encourages general interest stories, holiday photos, etc. It is not unusual for John himself to chime in on a particular subject of interest.

It's a truism that many of those responsible for decision-making of this kind are of older generations, and working in positions of responsibility where caution is a virtue. However, it's important to put concerns about new communication channels into perspective. I'm old enough to remember when email was first implemented. It seems anachronistic now to observe that email is a regular part of doing business, but at the time, I recall that many of our managers were afraid of the legal ramifications of electronic communication that could be sent to many people simultaneously. Social networks carry the same risks, but that is no reason not to use them. They're powerful tools. Generation Y lives in the era of instant and open communication; if we are going to be communicating with them and retaining them, we have to meet them where they live.

By all means, make sure your communications commitment plans for and covers any social networking tools that you choose to employ. And don't jump to implement one unless the follow-through is there; remember, your actions speak louder than words. Finally, if there are abuses – just as with email – meet with the individuals responsible offline, and remind them of the boundaries.

Of course, there is something to be said for the human touch. In addition to his blog, Paul Levy of Beth Israel Deaconess Medical Center makes a point of attending every orientation session in order to personally meet as many new hires as possible. But social networks can extend that human touch to realms that reinforce engagement, deepen trust, and create real change.

At a conference I recently attended, a presenter shared a great example of how social networks can be leveraged. An employee needed a bone marrow transplant, and doctors had been doubtful about the chances of finding a match. By leveraging a grassroots social network campaign that embraced the collective efforts of employees, vendors, and customers, the company located two matches. As of this writing, the employee is alive and well.

I think that even if you think long and hard, you'll find it difficult to come up with a story more likely to illustrate a company's commitment and care for its staff, as well as its ingenuity and fearlessness in leveraging new technologies.

The Importance of Innovation

Innovation is a key engagement driver. Employees want to create, be current, evolve, contribute new ideas and approaches, and work for the market leader. In his book *The Innovator's Dilemma*, Clayton Christensen points out that established companies asking a premium for their product or services must continue to innovate, because imitators, leveraging technology for lower costs or faster production, are bound to emerge offering something of similar or even lower quality (but good enough for the more mature company's customers)[28]. Unless a company can offer something of significantly greater value than this new competitor, they will be forced to compete on price – never a winning strategy. There are countless examples: the newspaper industry lost significant Help Wanted revenue from online competitors such as Monster and CareerBuilder, which undermined them on price. The cycle continues as these firms now worry about new job boards from Craigslist and LinkedIn. If you don't innovate, you will end up with an old model that can't compete.

[28]   Christensen, Clayton M. The Innovator's Dilemma. New York, NY: HarperCollins, 2003

Large film rental companies have been late to the game in streaming video and mail-order movies, just as the music industry has been sideswiped by iPod and iTunes. Even your local Certified Public Accountant (CPA) has had to innovate and offer financial planning services to combat the combined effects of (1) customers using Turbotax and (2) tax returns being outsourced to India. If you don't innovate, globalization and technology will starve you to death.

What are you doing to engage your employees by uncovering the potential for innovation that might exist in your own company? Does your culture underwrite creativity, or is it afraid of mistakes? Do risk-takers get punished? Companies that foster a higher level of expression from their employees (and that accept the fact that missteps are part of the creative process) are not only going to see more innovation – they're going to have more engaged employees.

Innovation can happen anywhere. One of the oldest occupations in the world is panhandling – sitting on a street corner or a train station, holding a cup. In New York City, however, one particular innovator has taken panhandling to the next level – strumming a guitar in his underwear in Times Square… and he's making a living.

One of the greatest and simplest innovative practices a company can embrace is job rotation – putting promising employees, especially at the junior level, onto tasks or into roles that may not have been part of their repertoire to date. Not only is this a prime means to foster engagement, it is difficult to overstate the value of having a very different set of eyes reviewing current processes, products, services, and structures. To foster continuous improvement, the architects of the present must submit to review by the residents, influencers, and innovators, of the future.

From the Trenches…

Although there are companies that offer a specific training investment to all employees (usually a specific number of training hours per year), I suggest this practice be avoided. Company-sponsored development is a privilege, not a right. An underperformer should not receive the same investment dollars as a top performer, and an employee with vast potential shouldn't receive the same level of training investment as an employee who has reached their potential.

Potential must be assessed. Some employees may simply require more training and investment than others. And don't forget the necessity to individualize your engagement, as discussed in Step 5. If a particular individual is fired up by the opportunity to develop new skills or improve existing ones, perhaps s/he is a candidate for future investment.

TOOLS + PROCESSES

Establish and Communicate Performance Norms

The purpose of engagement is to allow employees to reach their potential, while building a culture of high performance. However, if you don't define what it means to be average or what it means to be high-performing, it is unrealistic to expect any improvement from your employees. If I've learned nothing else studying employees over the past 29 years, it is this: employees want to win and don't want to be average! They want to excel! Most companies benchmark against their competitors, but shy away from benchmarking within their organization. You need to know who your top-performing 25% are in order to

learn why they perform highly. How do you define those individuals? What are their performance benchmarks? What is average, or sub-average, in terms of their business functions?

In conducting the bottoms up, high performance workshops that, at ENSR, we called "LEAP 2," I meet with the leadership team and share all of the metrics that have been gathered for assessment. On one occasion, I confronted a line manager whose business unit was dead average on every metric you could name: profitability, write-offs, business development, etc. But this man could not

believe that I wanted to share these results with his staff. "But they'll be demoralized to know that they're average!" he protested. "I hate to disappoint you," I told him, "but they *are* average, and they need to know it in order to improve." Why would an employee change if s/he thinks performance is already at a high level? The best you can expect, if you do not communicate average and high-performance norms, is to sustain mediocrity.

Once we started sharing metrics with that average business unit, the results were immediate. Stunned to know that they were C students, those employees immediately wanted to know what the high-performing units were doing differently. They met and collaborated, and came up with dozens of ideas on how to improve. Over time, they reached top 25% performance!

Establish a Corporate University

In creating a motivational culture, everybody wins. The company advances, and there are more bonus dollars, more training opportunities, and other tangible benefits, like the ability to attract the best employees to your firm. One means of sharing best practices (and of branding everything that you're doing to develop staff) is to create a corporate university.

This doesn't have to be a huge investment. In fact, a corporate university can be launched simply by collecting and branding all of the training, development, conferences, seminars, etc that are already in place. At ENSR, part of our University effort simply involved creating a calendar accessible on our intranet where key meetings, training opportunities, or conferences fell – be they related to business development, project management, administration, or actual project work. Any employee could open the calendar and see what was happening across the company, regardless of whether it related to their personal position or discipline. By encouraging people to reach out and share best practices, we kindled engagement and leveraged one of the best branding opportunities available.

I may forget to sweep the back deck for weeks on end, but if I make a point of letting my wife know that I did finish the dishes, take out the garbage, and clean the garage, I keep my reputation as a great husband and partner!

You don't have to increase your budget – just improve your means of capturing and communicating everything related to training. People throughout your company, regardless of its size, are participating in development and other admirable things! You must capture and market these back to your employees. Part of a leader's responsibility is to track what is happening at the office or departmental level. Part of it should also be reporting back, particularly with regards to new systems or practices from which others may learn.

Once you establish this branded framework, you can formalize your University with targeted training and development programs. The important thing is, you don't have to wait – in fact, you shouldn't. Talk up what you're already doing!

Once you embrace unpleasant news, not as a negative but as evidence of a need for change, you aren't defeated by it. You're learning from it.

– BILL GATES

STEP SEVEN
CREATE FEEDBACK MECHANISMS

If you are espousing a culture of open and honest communication, your policies and practices must include means for that to happen. Generally speaking, alignment is about getting two or more factions that are dependent on one another motivated so that they are all pulling toward the same goals. Of course, management is likely primarily focused on profit, sales, and brand performance, while individual employees' concerns may fall more into the categories of professional satisfaction, growth opportunities, or compensation ("What's in it for me?"). But as discussed in prior chapters, you can expect an increase in performance when you establish mutual commitment – a connection between individuals' goals and those of your organization.

One widely-quoted study showed that as of 2001, only 7% of employees reported that they fully understood their company's business strategies and what was expected of them in order to help achieve company goals[29]. In part, this disparity has historically had to do with misunderstanding on the part of executives, who may have equated engagement (and all of the commitments that go with it) with employee satisfaction, or who undervalue the need for effective, two-way communication (the waterfall and the fountain).

Having thorough feedback mechanisms in place is the only way to ensure that any engagement initiatives you've undertaken are the right ones, are progressing, and are embraced and supported by management and staff. A healthy feedback culture is also the best means to confirm and continuously re-establish trust between employees and management, and to tap the ideas that cannot help but emerge from an engaged culture.

Companies that establish a continuous feedback loop between management and employees virtually guarantee alignment. Leaders can lay the groundwork for engagement by frequently and enthusiastically expressing their mission and values, to ensure their employees are aligned. But without a means for employees to express their experiences, needs, recommendations, and how they're being led, it is unlikely that your engagement efforts will gain traction.

Establish a Communication Commitment

At ENSR, our first LEAP 2 workshops (see Step 2 for more on these) uncovered a significant communications gap. Employees were not receiving consistent messages. They didn't really know how the business was performing as a whole, or how their local business or department was performing in comparison. The LEAP 2 workshops also introduced the average and high-performing "norms" discussed in Step 6, in recognition of the fact that it is impossible to build a culture of high performance if employees are not aware of the performance expectations and of their standing in relation to those expectations. In response, the company developed a more rigorous internal communications program, which included new messaging about the company vision and business priorities, and included

---

29   Kaplan, Robert S. and Norton, David P. The Strategy-Focused Organization. Cambridge, MA: Harvard Business School Press, 2001

performance metrics on revenue growth, profit, employee engagement, client satisfaction, health and safety, and other topics. This was communicated through a new set of processes that came to be known as the Communication Protocol, which became one of our most crucial vehicles to communicate to employees and in turn, seek their feedback.

The Communication Protocol, or Commitment, outlines the types of information to be communicated to the organization, as well as identifying the person(s) responsible for communicating particular topics. In addition, the audience, frequency, and suggested communication vehicles are also outlined. Prominently displayed in all common areas such as lobbies and conference rooms, and distributed to all new hires, the Commitment ensures that communication serves the goal of keeping people informed, and aligning them with the company's key strategic priorities.

As importantly, the Commitment represents a set of company promises to employees, including:

- Leaders will be held accountable for fulfilling their communication responsibilities and assessed on the effectiveness and timeliness of their communication.

- Employees will receive regular updates about the progress, initiatives, and changes that affect them.

- And (most importantly for this step of the engagement process), each communication milestone provides opportunities for employees to ask questions, contribute ideas, and give or receive feedback.

In turn, the expectations for employees are clear. All employees are responsible for sharing information and giving feedback to help the company reach its goals, thereby reinforcing the desire for employees to communicate "up" and bolstering the mutual commitment shared by employer and employee.

Together with the Balanced Scorecard (see Step 9), the institution of the Communication Commitment changed ENSR's culture to one of mutual commitment and high performance. All new hires received a copy of the Commitment, demonstrating the company's promise to communicate on day one.

Create Your Own Communication Promise:

1. Message: List your specific strategic and measurable talking points (health and safety objectives, profit targets, client service, employee engagement metrics, etc.)

2. Who Delivers: Who is delivering the message? (CEO, Leadership Team, Division Manager, Office or Store Manager, Supervisor, etc.)

3. Venue (email, Town Halls, webinars, department meetings, etc.)

4. Frequency (Quarterly, Monthly, Weekly)

In the sample that follows, note that each category is divided into information and dynamic categories. The former simply mean to *communicate information* (waterfall); the latter aim to *solicit feedback* (fountain).

SAMPLE COMMUNICATION COMMITMENT

Scope	Message / Topic	Leader	Venue	Audience	Frequency
Communication of GENERAL Info, Designed to PROVIDE UPDATES					
Corporate	Company Update: • Review of company metrics (e.g. net sales growth, etc.) • Recent awards/opportunities • Organizational development update • International news • Recognition	CEO	Email	All employees	Quarterly / Monthly
Regional	Quarterly Review Meeting: • Review of company metrics (e.g. bus. development review, etc.) • Recognition • Organizational development update	Regional VP	On-site, conf. call, or WebEx meetings	All employees of region	Quarterly / Monthly
Office	Office Update: • Review of key metrics (e.g. performance to plan, net sales growth, etc.) • Recent Awards/Opportunities • Workload leveling • Recognition • Organizational development update	Office Manager	On-site, conf. call, or WebEx meetings	All employees of office	Monthly / Bi-weekly
Department	Workload leveling: • Recent Wins Proposal Activity • Prof. Development Opportunities • Health + Safety • Recognition		On-site meetings	All employees of department	Weekly / Bi-weekly

Scope	Message / Topic	Leader	Venue	Audience	Frequency
Communication of GENERAL Info, Designed to SOLICIT FEEDBACK					
Corporate	Company Update	CEO	Email	All employees	Monthly
Corporate	Strategy Update	Regional VP	On-site, conf. call, or WebEx meetings	All employees of region	Quarterly
Regional	Operations Review: • Performance vs. plan • Key account update • Strategic initiatives • Staff development update	Office Manager	On-site, conf. call, or WebEx meetings	All employees of office	Quarterly / Monthly
Communication of SALES Info, Designed to PROVIDE UPDATES					
Corporate	Service Lin/Industry Sectors: • Bookings + sales trends • Overall performance • Key Wins • Prof. development opportunities	Applicable Leader	Email / Intranet	All employees	Quarterly
Communication of SALES Info, Designed to SOLICIT FEEDBACK					
Corporate	Must-win opportunities	Sr. VP Sales	Conf. Call	Regional VPs	Bi-weekly
Regional / Office	Regional Bus. Dev.Review: • BD plan review • Account plan review • Sales training	Regional Directors	Conf. Call	Office Directors; Sr. Sales Staff	Monthly
Communication of CORPORATE ADMINISTRATIVE/HR Info, to PROVIDE UPDATES					
Corporate	Employer of Choice Review: • Prof. development update • Employer of Choice Committee updates	Director of HR	Email; quarterly news-letter	All employees	Bi-weekly
Corporate	Innovation Committee Update	VP Quality	Email	All employees	Quarterly
Corporate	Organizational Development Update	Director of HR	Quarterly news-letter	All employees	Quarterly
Corporate	Bi-weekly + Quarterly Newsletters	Marketing Department	Intranet	All employees	Bi-Weekly / Quarterly
Communication of BOARD OF DIRECTORS Info, Designed to SOLICIT FEEDBACK					
BOD	Performance Metrics: • Performance vs. plan • Forecast • Sales + marketing update • Employee engagement update	CEO	Conf. call	BOD members + guests	Quarterly
BOD	Bi-weekly Shareholder Update	CEO	Conf. call	Shareholders, Regional VPs, CFO	Bi-weekly

360-Degree Reviews

As discussed in Step 4, 360-degree reviews are another vehicle (growing in popularity) by which employees can provide feedback on the company and on their experience of individual leaders.

Although most would acknowledge the utility and richness of 360-degree reviews, it should come as no surprise that many managers resist undergoing the process. Inviting feedback from one's staff can be intimidating on both sides. This is why, when a company embarks on soliciting 360-degree feedback for the first time, complete anonymity is crucial to the process. I also strongly suggest that all feedback be filtered before it is passed on to the person being reviewed. And of course, those participating in the process should go through the necessary training to ensure they understand how to manage the process productively. If a company lacks trust, it may be helpful to outsource the 360-degree review process to a third party, or at least, to consider partnering with a third party technology provider. This often reduces fears on the part of staff about confidentiality.

The most effective 360-degree feedback is thoroughly filtered, contains both quantitative and qualitative data, assessed not by the party being reviewed, but by his or her supervisor. Think about it this way: if feedback went directly to the individual being reviewed, one nasty comment might keep a reviewee awake at night for weeks, no matter how thoroughly it was surrounded by praise. A supervisor, from an impersonal distance, can put that one negative comment into its proper context – a statistic, to be reviewed as a subset of the total comments.

The goal is to provide a clear and constructive portrait of any given individual in the organization, not to provide a platform for complaint or derision. In my experience, once a person has undergone his or her first 360-degree review, fears subside – and communication and trust often improve.

From the Trenches...

I was once fortunate to have an instructor who used a great metaphor to highlight the downside of surrounding one's self with yes-men. Dr. Magid Mazen, a graduate professor in the Sawyer School of Management at Suffolk University in Boston, used to say that healthy organizations "remove the walls so they can look at the plumbing." I have found this a very useful metaphor in describing the need for

feedback mechanisms within a company. After all, if you don't remove the walls, you can't know what may be crumbling behind them. Absent this type of culture, you risk hearing only what you want to hear, just like the naked Emperor in the famous Hans Christian Andersen story.

When you create feedback mechanisms, you have to accept the bad news along with the good. Some of the feedback you receive will be erroneous or irrelevant, but you have to create an environment in which people are comfortable speaking truth to power. Otherwise, all you are doing is creating a culture in which people tell you what you want to hear... not exactly a model for business excellence. I recall a

> **Too often, I have seen top-level executives get angry when receiving unflattering feedback. This attitude, especially when it's displayed in a public forum, will effectively stifle any benefits that might arise from staff opinion. Don't shoot the messenger!**

specific meeting, many years ago, in which another executive and I brought bad news to our CEO. He got angry at the two of us (the "messengers"), and stormed out of the room. My colleague simply said, "Well, that was uncomfortable – that's the last time I ever tell him something bad."

I went back to my office and sent the CEO (who worked in the office beside me) a one-sentence email. "If you get mad at people who tell you things you don't want to hear, they will stop telling you things, period." After a few hours, the CEO came into my office and said, "That was a valuable lesson for me – thank you!"

The LEAP 2 workshops discussed in Step 2 provide a communal, safe environment for feedback. You might be surprised at the ideas that emerge. I recall one workshop in particular where an attendee's manager had scoffed at the idea of a mass mailing to industrial clients in his area ("Too expensive, and these things don't work in our business.") But on reviewing his research (which he'd conducted independently, and which revealed over 5,000 potential clients within a hundred-mile radius) the junior level LEAP 2 participant's idea was voted the best they'd heard during the workshop.

The idea was implemented, new clients were uncovered, and backlog went up – all based upon an idea that never would have gained traction if its generator did not have a mechanism for marketing and gaining support for it. This is a good example why you shouldn't rely solely on the person in charge to evolve the business. Often, they are too vested in defending the present, and can have blinders on regarding new approaches.

TOOLS + PROCESSES

Innovation Box

I have never been a fan of the company "suggestion box." In my experience, these tend to become clogged with complaints, often of the pettiest sort. If management is responsive to such complaints, their response tends to support employee satisfaction, not employee engagement.

What you want is an *Innovation Box* – a feedback mechanism geared toward soliciting specific suggestions for innovation. How can we improve our proposal system? How should our technology evolve? Should our billing be centralized? What can we be doing better in terms of customer service? Are there new markets we need to penetrate? What technologies or products are we missing?

At ENSR, we formalized this process by adding an "Innovation Lightbulb" to our intranet homepage, and made it clear that we were looking for proactive, well-thought-out ideas on how our employees could help the company innovate. Everyone who sent in an idea was recognized for it, and rewarded with a small gift card. A committee, including members of the senior leadership team, reviewed all suggestions and responded to each submitter letting them know whether (and why) their idea was or was not

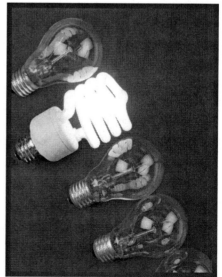

implementable. The cream of the crop were sent to the company's CEO. Many of these ideas made their way into our policy and processes, and even new and enhanced service offerings.

> **Solicit innovative ideas, not vague "suggestions." Too often these end up being along the lines of complaints.**

This is engagement at its best. An Innovation Box establishes a direct connection between the individual's contribution and the welfare of the organization as a whole. It further funds trust, and a sense that the individual is being heard. And perhaps most importantly, it provides a means by which new ideas – the fuel of a company's future – can flourish.

Social Media (Blogs, YouTube, Linkedin, Etc.)

In an attempt to leverage developments in social networking technologies, in the late 2000s many companies instituted blogs authored by their CEOs, presidents, or other top-level executives. This idea has considerable merit if the executive in question is truly committed to the idea and the process, and if the communications strategy incorporates checks and balances to ensure that both entries and comments are saying productive things. However, if an executive is not committed to blogging, or expects that his or her entries be ghostwritten or excessively vetted, a blog of this sort is ultimately of negative value. A disconnect will result between what the blog is saying and what the executive "knows," and once this is discovered, the credibility of the project – and of corporate communications as a whole – will be undermined.

Some companies with which I've worked have found that blogging, for mid- or junior-level staff to whom self-expression and new technologies are motivators, are a perfect vessel for discretionary effort. If a senior-level employee does not have the time or motivation to blog, consider spreading the responsibility among several mid-level employees who have a passion for it. Preferably, this would include a roster of bloggers who are representative of your firm's diversity in terms of discipline and cultural background, but you should recruit on the basis of passion and commitment first and foremost.

Paul Levy, CEO of Beth Israel Deaconess Medical Center in Boston, blogs regularly as part of his company's communication strategy. His *runningahospital.blogspot.com* is an examplar of open dialogue that reaches employees who might not otherwise read company missives.

As with all communications, your actions will speak louder than words. Don't over-commit to a blog, an electronic bulletin board, a YouTube channel, or a Twitter feed, and then not follow up. Recognize that you need to have the staff and resources to handle any new communications program, and that the popularity or "sexiness" of a new vehicle is not, in and of itself, sufficient justification for utilizing it.

One highly successful use of new technological avenues has come from the Deloitte company, which in recent years has moved away from company-produced videos toward user-generated content. With its own YouTube channel, Deloitte is exploiting a tremendous opportunity not only to brand themselves, but also to gather feedback. Each two-minute video, produced by staff, provides a glimpse into how employees view their place of work, and allows management to learn from the insights and experiences of those in the trenches.

Town Hall Meetings

All too often, whether impelled by a big announcement or the simple acknowledgement that it's time to touch base with staff, presidents or CEOs will tour their departments or offices accompanied by a full entourage (the CFO and COO, or worse, the complete leadership team). After delivering the necessary update in the form of a presentation or speech, that leader will then ask, "Are there any questions?"

I'm hard-pressed to think of a circumstance in which honest questions are *less* likely to result, or of one more likely to cement a divide between leadership and staff. Leaders often undervalue the length of the shadow they cast, and underestimate how important it is to staff to feel that leaders care. "Dropping by" the office with something to report, or under an obligation to fraternize, squanders the opportunity for dialogue.

Before you show up, leverage your resources to learn about the environment you'll be delving into. What are the specific concerns of your audience? Are they aligned with the overall company vision? Do they have firm ideas about where their jobs fit in? If presenting a specific issue or issues, solicit questions in advance; that way, if they are not brought up over the course of the meeting, you can address them anyway.

This is an opportunity to demonstrate that you're "all in this together." To that end, don't barricade yourself behind an entourage. Show up by yourself, or – better yet – team up with a junior-level colleague. You'll gain credibility, and so will they. Don't underestimate the value of one-on-one time with junior employees either. Instead of taking a cab or a limo to your destination, have the junior employee (or even a new employee) pick you up and chaperone the day. Their enthusiasm will likely be infectious, and their concerns may further inform your interactions with other staff.

> Don't forget to host Town Hall-style meetings in the corporate offices! Often, executives believe that because they share physical space with corporate-level employees, these people will learn about key messages via osmosis of some sort. Or perhaps the intentions are more strategic, with heavy outreach to non-corporate offices meant to offset the perception that corporate employees "get everything" and can communicate with executives whenever they want.
>
> As John Pazzani of Timberland says, "You have to win your home state first."

If you truly wish to solicit honest feedback, the key is to create a safe, low-key, informal environment, to the extent that that's possible. Rather than delivering a formal Powerpoint presentation, consider hosting a brown-bag discussion or "Town Hall" meeting moderated by a mid-level leader that staff know and trust. This may be uncomfortable at first for executives accustomed to the "safety blanket" of static, one-way communications, or to presenting with their "team" beside them, but it is one of the simplest and most direct feedback mechanisms available in modern corporate environments.

137

Employee Engagement Survey – Benchmarks

If engagement is a goal, naturally it is important to learn where you stand today in relationship to where you would like to be. And for that, you need a survey. High-performing organizations understand the need to survey their employees. Seventy-five percent (75%) of Aberdeen Group's top 20% organizations (those Aberdeen has identified as "Best-in-Class") have a standard process in place to measure engagement, such as engagement surveys – and this process is executed frequently[30]. Conversely, only

30% of Aberdeen's bottom-ranked do. However (and I cannot stress this in strong enough terms) do NOT embark on an employee engagement survey unless you are 100% committed to following up on what your employees tell you. You will lose more trust, and generate more cynicism, than if you never conducted a survey in the first place.

Even if this is your first survey of this sort, it is important to contrast your results against one or more benchmarks. If you look at individual departments or offices or business units' results in comparison with the company as a whole, that is an important "micro" comparison – the benchmarking against each other. Most survey companies will also provide benchmarks against other companies, which can be valuable for a number of reasons. It is important to note, for instance, that

---

[30] *Beyond Satisfaction: Engaging Employees To Retain Customers.* Aberdeen Group report, July 2009

Of course, if you have a culture of open, honest, and frequent communication, you will also get ongoing (and unsolicited) informal feedback. As Lisa Zankman, Beth Israel Deaconess Medical Center's Senior Vice President of HR, reminds us, "Because of who Paul Levy is, our employees are always giving us lots and lots of feedback!" Make sure your leaders are equipped to handle this inevitable consequence!

very few individuals respond with an unqualified affirmative to the question "Are you adequately compensated for your efforts." Therefore, if even 30% of your employees respond "Yes," with proper benchmarks, you might learn that this is actually a favorable score compared to like companies.

Even if the survey itself is designed to assess employee engagement, you need to compare the survey's results against high performance. What are high-performing companies' results for the same questions? Many survey consultants can provide you with those "macro" benchmarks, including comparing your results against your peer group and assessing your results against other high performing companies. Again, the goal is not to be average, but to evolve to sustained high performance.

Your baseline survey results then become your historical benchmarks. Many companies attempt an annual survey, but in my opinion this is a mistake. By the time survey results are corralled and reviewed by leadership, distributed internally, and acted upon, most companies will find that measurable progress will not occur until the following year. Changes will not have had time to propagate, and employees won't have had time to digest them and provide constructive feedback. You might be setting yourself up for negative results on your follow-up survey ("I've seen no change yet!"). I recommend conducting employee engagement surveys every 18 months to two years, with mini "pulse" surveys every year if specific issues require refinement.

Engagement surveys can also help you validate the results of your employee engagement efforts. Susan Monagham, Vice President of Employee Engagement at Cisco Systems, reveals that Cisco can now calculate that a 10% increase in employee engagement survey scores will correspond to a 5% gain in overall sales booking, resulting in $2 billion in potential added revenue. If you can measure engagement within your organization via surveys, you'll begin to see the connection between your engagement efforts and profitable growth.

Engagement surveys also allow companies to measure difficult-to-quantify "inclusion trends" within an organization. Although diversity statistics are easier to capture, Cisco Systems Chief Diversity Officer Marilyn Nagle knew she needed to quantify Cisco's inclusion efforts while also holding the company's leaders accountable for the broader definition of "inclusion." Nagle made sure that the following eight questions were included in Cisco's employee engagement survey as part of their "Inclusion Index:"

- My team has a climate in which diverse perspectives are valued.

- At Cisco, employees are treated with respect regardless of their job or level.

- Cisco's senior leadership team emphasizes the value of a diverse workforce.

- My manager ensures fair treatment for everyone on my team.

- I know how to address disrespectful behavior.

- I can succeed at Cisco without sacrificing aspects of my personality or culture.

- At Cisco, employees can voice their opinions without fear of retribution.

- At Cisco, people are rewarded according to their job performance and accomplishments.

Any business or industry that pays equal rewards to its goof-offs and eager beavers... will find itself with more goof-offs than eager beavers.

– MICK DELANEY

STEP EIGHT
REINFORCEMENT, REWARDS
+ CONSEQUENCES FOR BEHAVIORS

In business, as in parenting, you'll find that you get the behavior that you measure and then reinforce. If you claim that training and development is of strategic importance, for example, you have to state the end goal (to create alignment), measure it (to create accountability) and then have consequences (positive or negative) for achievement compared to those measurements. Rewards (bonuses, raises, promotions, perks, and the like) must be dependent upon an individual's accomplishments measured against the goalposts. Conversely, if an individual is out of alignment (in the case of training and development, if, say, a profit center manager is foregoing his training obligation in order to improve the "bottom line"), there must be a consequence (reduction in bonus, raise, or career advancement) if you expect behavior to change.

This is the essence of business actions speaking louder than words. The company's actions must match up with what it is telling its employees if it wishes to create engagement rather than just "satisfaction."

Money as a Motivator/De-Motivator

Some people, in select functions such as commission-based sales, might be highly motivated by money. But in my experience, this is the exception. For the vast majority of people in any job, the more critical driver is achievement: they want to know that they are doing well. As discussed throughout this book, transparency in measurement is in and of itself an engagement factor. For behavior change, employees need to know how they are personally performing, how their business unit or department is performing, and how that relates to the performance of the company as a whole. This is why I've become adamant about the need to introduce a balanced scorecard (as explained in Step 9).

As a metaphorical exercise to introduce a workshop module on motivation, I will sometimes have senior executives work in teams to construct paper airplanes, and then participate in a contest to see which team's plane will fly the farthest or stay aloft longest. During the contests, you would be surprised to see these groups of often serious-minded, buttoned-down businesspeople excitedly cheering on their team's effort. (Screams and high-fives are not at all uncommon.) Afterwards, I ask, "Why were you behaving like that over a paper airplane contest, knowing that you weren't going to be paid any money or receive any prize if you won?" The

answers I get, and the expressions on the group's faces, indicate that this amusing little team-building game has demonstrated a truth that many bottom-line-oriented

executives rarely think about: people don't *want* to under-achieve. Achievement – not money or prizes – is its own motivating engagement driver.

Of course, most employees would never explicitly admit that money does not motivate them. On surveys, ratings for "I am adequately compensated," are consistently low across all industries, and with all companies. No one wants to give their company a license to cut pay or to reduce raises. But it should be noted that while money is not a primary driver of engagement, it can certainly disengage staff if they feel they're being rewarded unfairly compared to others internally to the company or externally.

As a follow-up to the paper airplane exercise, I'll often ask that same group of executives two questions. "If I gave each of you $5,000 tomorrow, in two or three weeks, would you be working any harder?" Most, being honest with themselves, would have to say no. (Although at least one per session usually jokes, "Well, give us the money and we'll let you know.") Conversely, "If I cut your salary by $5,000 tomorrow, in two or three weeks, would you be less engaged?" In this case, it's easy for the executives to see why there would be erosion in engagement.

Generally speaking, a good model for an engaged culture is to pay at or slightly above the midpoint in total compensation (and to offer the industry standard or slightly better in benefit programs), but to offer greater sharing in the company's overall gains (whether that means larger bonuses and/or profit sharing). The reasons this model works should be apparent by now: it reiterates the engagement theme of mutual commitment by the company and the individual employee. It not only says "When we win, we win together..." it proves it. Additionally, firms that cautiously manage their fixed payroll costs (i.e. base salaries) while allowing for greater upside in the variable component (bonuses and profit sharing), will better survive a "down" year.

Measurements as Engagement Tools

Measurement is key to showing that engagement leads to improved performance, and to strengthening that feedback loop. Historically, the gold standard of HR metrics has been voluntary turnover (and the information obtained in exit interviews) because, in contrast to many "soft" measurements, it is a quantitative data point. However, although this metric is important, it is assessing disengagement retroactively – it is trailing, not leading information.

While qualitative measurements are essential (more on this later), it is crucial to establish more proactive "hard" or quantitative data about the state of engagement at your company. This can consist of an increase or deterioration in employee engagement survey scores, in the number of employee referrals, in training and development participation, and in client satisfaction metrics, to name some powerful examples. These data points can then be compared alongside profit and growth numbers for a clear picture of their correlation.

Non-Tolerance for Non-Conformance

Even in an engaged culture, there will likely be times when management will be faced with a tough decision about a top performer (whether that's a top profit or sales producer, top client liaison, or top technical specialist) who isn't subscribing to the same standards for engagement as the business. When it comes to values and shared operating principles, firms need to take a no-tolerance position on non-conformance, regardless of who the non-conformer is or of his or her success in other areas. If, for example, it is part of a company's values and stated commitment to staff to give regular feedback, and a single manager consistently disregards the Communication Commitment directing how, when, and how often feedback is to be given, that manager is falsifying the company's commitment. Consequences (or lack thereof) for such behavior will speak louder than words.

When ENSR began to measure succession planning, we made it clear to our managers that we would hold them accountable for their responsibilities regarding performance reviews (one of our key qualitative metrics). For years, getting them to complete, document, and submit their employee reviews on time had been a consistent problem. We'd tried rewarding those who hit their marks, but this was a classic case of money not being a motivator – the problem did not go away. Ultimately, we realized that our system lacked accountability in the form of consequences for non-conformance. And amid some protest, we instituted a new policy: anyone who did not complete his or her reviews on time would not get a year-end bonus or pay increase. Response to the review deadline increased

dramatically, almost immediately. (Of course, we then had to make sure that the measurement was "performance reviews done correctly" rather than just "done.")

In this case, it's important to recognize that while the consequences were monetary, the key to the new policy's success was the measurement combined with the consequence, which defined the goal and the individual's achievement relative to it. Although there may be some grumbling at first, persist in taking the hard line.

Rewards are the byproduct of successful achievement, but if there is no consequence for underachievement, there will be no behavior change. This is true regardless of what you are measuring, whether it is quality of service, mentorship, or engagement.

Total Compensation Programs That Work (and Those That Don't)

When it comes to compensation, employees are masterful at figuring out how to game the system. Be careful what you measure. If all of your measurements are quantitative – where the employee knows "If I meet the following number, I will get X reward" – they may meet the numbers in ways that are not in the company's best interests. If bonuses or pay increases are solely based on profit, your budgets for innovation and training won't be used. Your staff will be too busy trying to maximize their numbers to "waste time" on creativity or developing their careers… two things that are vital to a company's future.

At ENSR, earlier bonus plans rewarded leaders based primarily on the performance of his or her local business unit, which created an island mentality. ("Why should I share work or resources with anyone else? That's going to dent my bonus.") Recognizing this, we changed the plan so that the first indicator of bonus size was overall company performance. A single business unit could have a great year. But if the whole company didn't do well, the difference between an individual's bonus and that of a colleague in a different region (whose office was perhaps behind in revenue or backlog) might be negligible.

Here's where businesses are unique, and need to take the time to determine the behaviors and traits they are trying to encourage to reach their goals. Is it positive attitude? Volunteering to mentor? Eagerness to take on stretch assignments? Those are all things for which you can set goals, create accountability, and (if warranted) reward. Measure them!

The tie to overall company performance and compensation once again underscores the message that "we're all in this together." However, if you think about it, it makes sense for one's tenure and level to play into the equation. The more junior a person is, the less his or her compensation should be dependent upon overall company performance – a short time with the company may not yet warrant trust in mutual commitment. For junior staff, it is better for rewards to be based more heavily on local achievements (be that within a team or department or business unit), and to be given more frequently, to underscore the link between the particular achievement and the reward. For senior employees – executives and managers – the link to overall company performance should be much more explicit, and the rewards (while larger) should follow more infrequently. This arrangement creates incentives for high performance throughout an organization's hierarchy.

> Some of your metrics for compensation must be qualitative: teamwork, employee engagement, or business development activity (not just sales). How much work did you export? Did you import staff? How well did you train?

Compensation and bonuses, also, must be closely correlated to the potential to grow and learn. A satisfied employee doing a decent job who shows no interest in advancement or training should eventually "max out" his or her salary – it might not be in the company's best interests to continue investing in that person. In these instances, bonus or variable pay is the more appropriate incentive to maintain that mid-level of engagement.

TOOLS + PROCESSES

Compensation Matrix

You want to pay for performance, but perhaps you're wondering "How do I spend a 3% merit pool for maximum engagement?" Often, managers fail to use such budgets to make the appropriate distinction between average and exceptional performance. This isn't T-Ball – everyone does not deserve the same trophy.

If you dole out 2.5% to underperformers, 3% to average performers, and 3.5% to top performers, you may discourage your top performers while giving underperformers no incentive to improve. The "peanut butter" approach to incentive pay is sloppy. Don't use "number of employees" as the denominator for your pay increase or bonus pool and just spread it around. The same 4-quadrant matrix discussed in Step 1 is a handy tool for determining rewards. For compensation or bonuses, plot employees into the four quadrants, based on performance and potential, with "X" being average award.

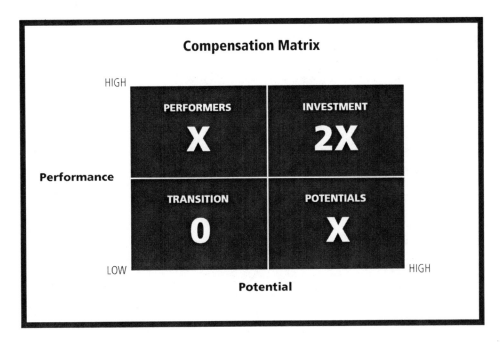

Transition employees should not be rewarded, and investment employees should receive no less than 2x average. Between performers and potentials, give the edge to potentials – they are likely to be new or junior staff, for whom the slight boost will be more closely tied to specific, recent achievements.

Decouple Development Planning from Compensation

As mentioned above with regards to making compensation work to reinforce the right behaviors, it is critical that qualitative and quantitative criteria be explicitly spelled out and made part of each employee's development plan. However, whatever those criteria are, it is important to avoid implying what reward to expect by meeting or exceeding each measurement. There are two reasons for this. First, by dangling a carrot, you're virtually ensuring that employees will reach only that far. Secondly, if at all possible, you should decouple any performance review from the issue of salary. As discussed in Step 5, too many review processes spend too much time on *what* the employee is doing without touching on *why*. The employee development plan and ensuing conversations should spend as much time if not

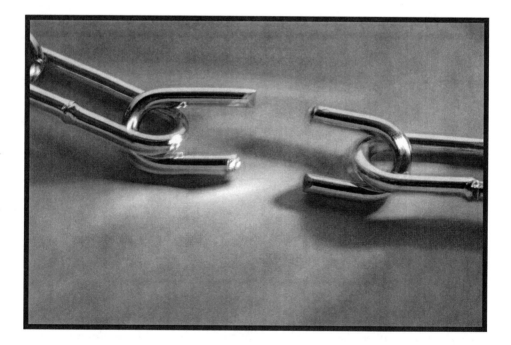

more on the future trajectory of the individual's career. Otherwise, throughout the review, the employee will be sitting there wondering what his or her pay increase is going to be – not a particularly productive state of mind for thinking much farther than a month down the road.

Whenever your salary increases generally occur (traditionally at the end or beginning of the year), my recommendation is to schedule employee development plans (or performance reviews) in an off-season. That way, when it comes time to discuss a pay increase (or lack of one), you have months of performance to underwrite your communication of why the figure is as it is. And at the least, you've now built in two times a year when a manager formally meets with his/her employee to discuss performance and future goals.

However beautiful the strategy, you should occasionally look at the results.

– WINSTON CHURCHILL

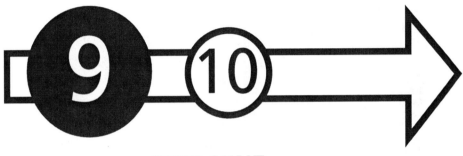

STEP NINE
TRACK + COMMUNICATE PROGRESS + SUCCESS

When my kids were young, my wife and I sometimes took them for a Sunday drive to look at the New England autumn foliage. Perhaps predictably, we discovered that children are not into scenery, and suffered through chants of "Are we there yet?" I still remember my wife responding, "There is no there." Meaning there is no destination – we're taking a drive and then returning home.

Because the rewards of an engaged culture are numerous and enduring, many leaders reading this book may be tempted to make engagement an action item to get "there" right now. There's nothing wrong with that enthusiasm, but it needs to be tempered by the sober realization that any kind of cultural change is a multiple-year process. I like to refer to engagement as "a journey with no destination:" (there is no there). Your engagement journey will

continuously change, and you should never be satisfied with "arriving." You will need to continuously monitor and evolve where you – and your employees – are going.

Before beginning on any efforts to improve employee engagement at your organization, you need to accept that tangible results may not be immediately forthcoming. The investments you'll be making will take time to take root and grow. As discussed in previous steps, developing a system of measurement will reassure you about the results of specific actions. But if you're hoping to check off a box marked "employee engagement" for Year X and then move on to the next important thing, you won't only disappoint yourself – you'll engender cynicism about the entire process in your staff. And cynicism is corrosive to engagement.

Once you publicly announce your commitment to any engagement-related measure as part of your business strategy, you must be forthright about the evolutionary character of what you are trying to accomplish. In order to set expectations appropriately (and fend off pessimism at the outset), be honest about your goals with staff, and let them know exactly what you'll be tracking, how the outcomes will be communicated back, and how they can help. The promise that you are making is an important part of building trust, allegiance, and alignment.

The mistake some companies make is that if they don't see immediate results, they move on to something else. Accept from the outset that your initiatives might take one to two years to show their desired effects. Also, accept that you will never be able to say, "Well, we're done with engagement. Now on to quality control, customer service, etc."

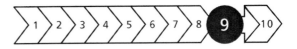

As Jim Collins points out in *Good to Great* , leaders need to understand the power of "AND.[31]" Engagement is not "either / or" (e.g. we need to focus on engagement or quality this fiscal year). It needs to be *in addition to* other key business drivers. I believe most leaders know this, intuitively. However, if there is an economic hiccup, or a business downturn, engagement efforts often become the music department of a school system – the first to be cut for the fiscal year.

"Are We There Yet?"

Perhaps, instead of calling engagement a journey with no destination, it's worth noting that in a healthy organization the destination will continue to change. As you gauge the success of your initiatives, you will find that some needs have been fulfilled while new ones are emerging. At ENSR, one of the initial engagement goals was to improve work/life balance, which we tackled by building in new workplace flexibilities. Contrary to the predictions of a couple of our leaders, productivity went up, and as we watched engagement scores soar on that topic, it became clear that we no longer needed to focus our attentions 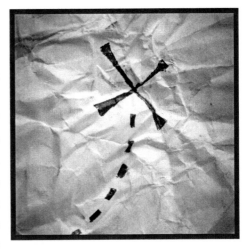 on work/life balance (although it would, of course, continue to be monitored). Our task – the task of any growing, evolving organization – then became to figure out what the next focal point should be.

The journey doesn't meander; it takes companies with purpose from point to point, creating a roadmap along the way. But it must resist complacency. There is always a goal to be set, measured, and communicated, and – if your organization fosters innovation – always another stop along the road.

Brand Your Successes

As discussed in Step 4 and throughout this book, targeted, open, and frequent communication is the crucial connective element without which any other

---

[31]   Collins, James C. Good to Great. New York, NY: HarperCollins, 2001

efforts at engagement will fail. As you are launching new initiatives, there will be changes and there will likely be failures. It's important to communicate all of these consistently, transparently, and well. But above all, you must "toot your own horn." Your staff's desire to be proud of the place they work will subsidize and perpetuate your successes, regardless of what those are. Never forget that your employees want to work for a winner – success breeds success.

Even at the very beginning, when results from a new initiative may be thin or not quite as you'd hoped, take the time to locate the quick wins. Where are you succeeding? It doesn't matter if the successful program or event doesn't coincide precisely with recent strides in employee engagement. If your company as a whole, or any of its subdivisions, has seen positive results with a product, program, or process, you need to broadcast that story as broadly as possible, using whatever channels are available to you. Topics that you may think are widely known may very well not be. Don't worry about being redundant if you are discussing something previously covered, or if your communications strategy includes coverage on your company intranet, in Town Hall-style meetings, and in the form of executive emails or corporate newsletters. For every individual who has seen two of these venues, there will be three who've seen none. There is no such thing as overcommunicating a success.

Be Ambitious, But Realistic

In Step 2, I mentioned the important point that engagement is not free. The key in communicating your investments to staff is in identifying the three or four items that you can realistically commit to in Year One as part of a five-year plan; budgeting for them; and measuring their success. Enthusiasm is all well and good, but don't be overly ambitious in either your goals or your communication, because shortfalls will be noticed and can engender cynicism. Remember: keep it simple and execute it flawlessly.

What investments are you going to make? If you're going to increase training from 4% to 6% of payroll, what exactly is that expenditure meant to achieve? What is the improvement within the business? Also, as discussed in Step 8, what are the indicators or correlatives for investment? What are the goals – more internal advancement and succession candidates, or increase in innovation? Improvements

in overall engagement scores? Define and track your engagement initiatives as you would any other investment, and don't hesitate to ask the hard questions. Are you seeing the improvements that you expected? If not, why not? Have you given the investments enough time to grow? Are you investing enough? And make sure your employees understand that dollars are finite: that the organization has other priorities that also need investment.

Break it Down

It's not enough to simply say, "Employee engagement is of critical importance to this company. We're going to invest in it and measure it." Even if you have the best intentions, from your staff's standpoint this sounds like hot air because it is too broad. Chances are that they suspect the challenges your organization faces and will appreciate your acknowledgement of the specific mileposts that will help resolve them.

By the time you make any announcement of this sort, you should have identified your goals and decided upon how they will be measured, tracked, and reported. If you want to reduce turnover to single digits, tell your staff not only that this is an objective, but also how your performance and progress will be tracked. If your goal is to have 50% of new hires to come from employee referrals, tell your staff what the benchmarks are both within your company and against competitors, if those are your metrics.

Sharing your plan in detail gives your message credibility up front – employees can see the extent of thought and preparation that has been devoted to the specifics. This makes a much stronger impression than airy proclamations like, "Employees are our greatest asset." When you then follow up on these messages, you supplement your credibility much more than if you had reported successes that were not explicitly tied to your goals.

Metrics Are Unique to Your Organization

There is no cookie-cutter approach to identifying metrics, since they have to flow from your company's goals. If you have quality or client satisfaction issues because of voluntary turnover, you need to look at how voluntary turnover breaks down in relationship to your staff population. High turnover of the disengaged or low-performing, after all, is not necessarily a bad thing, but if you are losing a lot of high-potential or high-performing people, that's clearly a problem, and you need to learn the underlying causes or specific location. With turnover, you can also look for correlations in tenure or diversity. Are you losing predominantly new employees? Is turnover different between men and women? Between your Gen Y employees and your boomers? You may also need to benchmark against cultural yardsticks that transcend your company. For example, turnover in Asian countries is typically far lower than in the West – so low turnover at an enterprise in Tokyo might not be significant measured against statistics for an organization with a multinational presence. Is it low not just in comparison to the rest of the company, but compared with Asian companies in general?

> In my experience, the question of engagement versus profits is often a chicken-or-egg scenario. You cannot sustain a healthy business without both. If you have high engagement but no profit, your engagement will suffer – no one wants to be part of a losing business. But if you have profits without engagement, watch that figure – it will likely be short-lived.

At ENSR, we learned that extraordinary client satisfaction without engagement was impossible. But we also learned that to improve engagement scores (and retention), we had to focus on smaller, more concrete goals, and find quantitative means to measure them. Earlier, I mentioned work/life balance as a goal that we went about achieving by building flexibility into the workday. We began to measure the number of employees who were telecommuting for part of the work week (and of course, we modified our policies to encourage and accommodate this new trend). We also had goals to increase the percentage of our employees who were "complementary" (non-full time), and even began to offer health benefits for part time employees to accommodate those who wanted more work/life balance.

These metrics then had to be correlated with business metrics. In the case of ENSR, there was a clear link between client satisfaction, repeat business, and low turnover of engaged staff that reinforced the business reason for our engagement efforts.

Take the time up front to determine the metrics that make the best sense for the goals you are trying to accomplish. This sort of advance planning is the only way to make the most of your efforts to initiate engagement… and drive performance.

When In Doubt, "Overcommunicate"

I've said it before: no one ever quit an organization because of too *much* communication. Too often, managers will abdicate, assuming that because one communications channel has been leveraged, the job is done. "It's on the intranet. Why do I need to send a separate message out to my team?" The reason, in this instance, is that employees usually visit a corporate intranet when they are looking for something in particular. They're busy! For the most part, they don't spend their downtime browsing archives of company communications. Certainly, the information needs to be there and accessible – but that does not absolve line managers or executives from fulfilling their roles in the communications commitment (described in Step 7). Think of your intranet as a library – where information is stored, not where information is communicated.

Key messages, especially those having to do with progress or success, need to be queued and pushed out with the highest possible degree of frequency. Such communications are not only an opportunity to reiterate, but also to link the macro to the micro – to answer the question "How does this affect me?" A lazy approach won't cut it. You need to be proactive and specific. In addition to the intranet coverage or the monthly balanced scorecard (see page 161), layer on other communications wherever possible. Organize question-and-answer sessions. Distribute emails from the CEO or President. Touch on the issue at hand in weekly staff gatherings and call for feedback. What may seem tedious or redundant to you will often capture that one significant individual's attention for the first time, or in a whole new way.

From the Trenches…

Time and time again, I've seen the way that tracking and communicating progress underpins successful business operations. In one case where a business had been struggling, replacing a regional manager who was reluctant to communicate business results to employees with one who was tenacious about it was a $2 million difference! The region went from losing a million dollars per year to making a million dollars a year!

The previous manager had thought he was shielding his employees by protecting them from bad news, but by doing so he failed to create any impetus for change or any channel for constructive input from the ranks. By starting a frank conversation ("These are the goals. This is how we're doing. What do you think we should do to improve performance?"), the new manager tapped into his staff's innate urge to be competitive and to excel. Engagement scores, revenue growth, and profitability all improved.

As I've reiterated throughout this book, there has to be an alignment of message at all levels in order for engagement to thrive. If some managers are not tracking or communicating the things that the top level deems important, those managers are undermining the principles of engagement and threatening the long-term health of the business. Do not allow personal biases or preferences to determine how your communications commitment is executed!

To offer another example, a particular business outside the U.S. learned that its employee referrals had severely fallen off within recent years. The manager offered many excuses for why this was the case: it was a "cultural difference" that rendered referrals irrelevant; the budget to incentivize referrals could be better spent on marketing; it was more expedient to hire candidates without worrying about their provenance, etc. However, a cross-sectional workshop revealed that employees wanted to institute a referral goal, reward for it, and track it – and when bonuses were instituted, hiring success and retention skyrocketed.

Get down to the truth, and don't accept excuses. Seek feedback from employees in a variety of formats to determine what needs to be done for the health of the business. They are paying attention, and they want to succeed as much as you do.

TOOLS + PROCESSES

The Balanced Scorecard

As touched upon in Step 1, a Balanced Scorecard report – used to track staff activities that are both financial and non-financial in nature, and their results – has become a standard component of the modern business's toolkit. These reports generally derive from the company's strategy and goalposts,

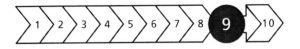

with measurements reflecting status in relationship to those goals. The Balanced Scorecard, in essence, provides a snapshot of the performance of an individual, a department, a business unit, or the entire company as compared to its objectives. Perhaps more than any other tool, a properly-executed Balanced Scorecard can create and support "line of sight" for employees.

A simplified sample scorecard is provided below. Note that the design of the card should be tailored to the company's goals for training, profit etc. Some of the most successful deployments of the Balanced Scorecard that I have seen reside on the company intranet, with users having the ability to sort the data by their personal performance or the performance of their department, office, or region.

Metric	Actual for Month	Plan for Month	YTD Actual	YTD Plan	Operations	Top 25%
Health + Safety						
OSHA Recordables	0	0	0	0	3	0
Lost Time Cases	0	0	0	0	2	0
Employee Engagement						
Traning % of Payroll	1.8	2.9	1.9	2.8	2.5	2.8
Turnover %: Voluntary	1.5	8.0	4.7	8.0	9.4	5.2
Turnover %: Involuntary	0.0	0.0	0.0	0.0	1.6	3.0
Employee Engagement Survey Favorable Rating %	88	100	88	88	78	89
Profitability						
Total Utilization %	71.6	68.4	64.3	67.5	62.2	68.8
Contribution Margin ($000)	384	415	1,477	1,735	20,606	1,188
Contribution Margin (% of Net Sales)	51.7	54.3	51.9	54.3	55.0	57.4
Operating Profit ($000)	115	123	298	548	6,539	566
Operating Profit % of Net Sales	15.5	16.0	10.5	17.1	17.5	29.0
Revenue Growth						
Proposal Backlog ($000)	2,550	0	2,550	0	58,863	3,166
Bookings ($000)	1,166	1,202	4,785	4,807	60,510	3,275
Project Backlog ($000)	4,509	4,000	4,509	4,000	87,111	5,281
Net Sales ($000)	744	765	2,844	3,199	37,454	2,112
Net Yield Multiplier x Total Utilization	2.01	2.03	1.81	2.00	1.87	2.20
Cost Management						
Total Facilities ($)	660	629	2,644	2,588	2,042	1,593
Total Discretionary ($)	442	447	1,671	1,764	2,123	1,817

Hire for intelligence and judgment, and most critically, a capacity to anticipate, to see around corners. Also look for loyalty, integrity, a high energy drive, a balanced ego, and the drive to get things done.

– COLIN POWELL

STEP TEN

HIRE + PROMOTE ENGAGED EMPLOYEES FOR YOUR CULTURE

Ernest Shackleton's famous Antarctic exploration is considered by many to be the greatest survival story of all time. I happen to think it is also one of the greatest hiring stories. In 1914, famed Antarctic explorer Ernest Shackleton selected 27 men to accompany him to Antarctica, with the extraordinary goal of crossing that continent on foot. Shortly after reaching the Antarctic, Shackleton's ship, the *Endurance*, was trapped in ice. She drifted aimlessly across the treacherous Weddell Sea for 10 months before being crushed by

the ice and sinking. Shackleton and his men floated on melting ice for months on end, before having to board their three small lifeboats in search of land.

Shackleton's extraordinary leadership skills kept the crew focused on their new goal: to stay alive. This survival story lasted approximately two years, and became famous for the success of its revised goal – not a single life was lost!

There is hardly a clearer metaphor for "we're all in this together" than this timeless story of survival. I believe that Shackleton's hands-on, empathetic leadership style represents one of the first and most successful examples of true engagement. He knew when to communicate a changed vision, telling his crew, "My new goal is to keep you alive." He knew when an authoritative leadership style should be supplemented by an altruistic one, often being the first to take the pick in hand to break up the ice, or to offer to exchange his dry mittens for a crewman's wet ones. He knew when to demonstrate succession planning, often rotating men to different assignments on the *Endurance* – unheard of in exploration sailing in 1914. But perhaps most importantly, he knew how to hire people to fit the enterprise he was running. The ad he published to recruit for his expedition ran as follows:

> **Men Wanted for Hazardous Journey.** *Small wages, bitter cold, long months of complete darkness, constant danger. Safe return doubtful. Honour and recognition in case of success.*

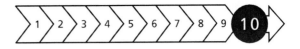

One certainly couldn't claim to have been misinformed about the nature of the job from its outset! Yet out of 5,000 candidates, Shackleton selected the very 27 whose behaviors and traits enabled him to lead them through extreme conditions from which all emerged alive. It is easy to imagine, in such a radically distilled example, how the traits associated with low performance (negativity, pessimism, a "me first" attitude, a focus on the monetary worth of individual tasks) could have spurred desertion, mutiny, or murder. But among his other leadership qualities, Shackleton recognized that hiring the right kinds of people for the rarified culture of his expedition was critical to its success.

Once you've identified your engagement differentiators, as discussed in Step 5, it's also important to incorporate them into your interview and selection processes. Are you hiring the right people for your company's culture – the ones most likely to be aligned with its goals and to apply their education and skills to its future? Conversely, if turnover is high, isn't it time to infuse your hiring procedures and inject a little more Shackleton-style analysis and rigor?

Externally Brand "Who You Are"

In Step 4, I discussed branding your company's successes and advantages internally. But of course, the power of branding extends far beyond "preaching to the choir." I believe that any organization's marketing team needs to be working in partnership with its staffing and resource teams to co-brand and co-publicize messages internally and externally. This is the means by which you will entice the best recruits and make the strongest and best impression on potential new clients.

Ernest Shackleton's "Help Wanted" ad demonstrates why having the reputation of an Employer of Choice is critically important for your business. When one first reads Shackleton's ad, it is difficult to imagine how he was able to solicit 5,000 inquiries – after all, the job he's offering doesn't seem to offer many perks aside from the possibility of accomplishment against very difficult odds. However, by the time Shackleton was looking to staff the *Endurance* expedition, he had become a brand. He had built a stellar reputation as the leader of the 1907 Nimrod Antarctic expedition of 1907, and after establishing in January 1909 a southern altitudinal record (having travelled farthest to the south of the globe), he was knighted by King Edward VII.

I'll say it again: people want to work for a winner. By 1912, Shackleton had become a market leader, and hence was able to attract 5,000 candidates from which to select the best 27. By contrast, when he was looking to staff the Nimrod expedition (before he was a market leader), he was only able to attract a few hundred men.

Even during the peak years of staff shortages (the "The War for Talent" years, immediately following the 9/11 tragedy), General Electric, Google, Southwest Airlines, Microsoft, and other employers of choice in their respective industries had ample candidates to choose from.

When the talent and job network *monster.com* was in its early stages its founder, Jeff Taylor, had the vision to invest in branding in one of the most visible of all U.S. venues: Super Bowl advertising. The stakes were high (the company was not yet profitable, and certainly didn't have much money for commercials), but Taylor saw the potential rewards of running an ad in one of the most widely-viewed broadcast events in the country, and went for it. The advertisement was seen by millions of people, and helped to cement *monster.com* as the go-to for job seekers, employers, and employees alike.

Is your brand able to attract the best?

What are you doing to promote your business as a winning proposition? As with your other goals related to engagement, you need to set goals, measure and communicate them, and pursue them in a highly visible way. If you are seeking to enter the Top 100 Places to Work, you need to apply to the organizations and news outlets responsible for making that designation. Even if you do not win the first time around, be committed to telling your employees and the rest of the world that you're a great place to work. Through repetition and follow-up, your employees, customer base, and applicant pool will begin to believe it. Never underestimate the fact that your employees want to work for a great employer.

For a sustainable branding model, you have to be not only telling your people that you're great, but telling the outside world as well. How and why are you great? If you ask your employees, the answer may surprise you. At AECOM, the common

In the mid-2000s, Cisco Systems struggled to establish a reputation with its employees and its marketplace as a diversity leader. But when CEO John Chambers became the face of inclusion and diversity for the company, Cisco saw immediate and ongoing gains in this area. Diversity Officer Marilyn Nagle remembers when the idea took hold: Chambers shared his personal experiences as a child and his passion for diversity during a global "virtual fireside" chat with all employees. When in 2009 the prestigious Diversity Best Practices organization awarded Chambers "CEO Champion of Diversity," his example proved again that engagement starts at the top, and that leaders' actions speak louder than words.

perception was that that people wanted to work there because of the company's reputation for technical excellence. And although technical excellence was and continues to be the cornerstone of AECOM's business, the 2006 employee engagement survey revealed that a top engagement driver for the majority of its employees was – surprise – working for a socially responsible employer. They worked at AECOM in order to help make the world a better place to work and live!

Technical excellence in the architecture, planning, and engineering fields was essential but simply a means to an end – the equivalent of "education and skills" in the BEST (Behaviors, Education, Skills, and Traits) profile. What really motivated the AECOM staff was commitment to a cause larger than their day-to-day work or their biweekly paycheck. AECOM shifted its branding focus to leverage this newly discovered engagement driver, and even now reinforces it with its stated purpose: "To enhance and sustain the world's built, natural, and social environments."

If your employees are succeeding based on a strong internal driver, this driver is precisely what you need to publicize if you want to hire the people who are most likely to be the right fit for your culture. This is the final means of ensuring perpetuity for engagement.

Back in Step 3, I touched on the irony that in hiring, often too much emphasis is placed on education and skills, and not nearly enough on behaviors and traits, despite the fact that the things that make for a great employee or a poor one fall into the latter two categories. Who are the winners in your environment? Who are the people that get promoted, not just hired?

Identify your company's top 10% — what behaviors and traits do they share?

To determine what behaviors and traits are most important for your culture, gather together a cross-sectional group of leaders with flipcharts and whiteboards and come up with the names of the employees who consistently embody excellence at your company. (The actual number of names will be dependent on the company's size – target the top 10%). It doesn't matter how junior or senior they are, or whether they are from R+D, retail, finance, HR, or development. Then start listing the behaviors and traits that make these individuals shine. Be careful to limit your list to personal qualities rather than achievements. Let's say John comes up with the best numbers. Why? Is it because he's a great architect (which you could attribute to education and skills)? No, it's because he's tenacious, creative, and resourceful (traits). He surrounds himself with the best people; he chases clients the company never would have pursued otherwise; he modifies his business development plan to incorporate new findings; he is tenacious in following up and following through (behaviors).

If these people on your list all have 15 consistent behaviors or traits that overlap, these are the tested, tried, and proven distinguishing characteristics for which you should be hiring. Of course education and skills are important (The E and S in BEST) but those are merely what's needed to get a candidate's foot in the door or to suggest adequate performance. You don't want adequate – you want excellent.

Hiring means that there is a void you're looking to fill – but the process of knowing who to hire is complex. Once you have identified the behaviors and traits for which you wish to hire, you will need to map these into your interviewing process. Your existing interview process may stress past assignments and accomplishments

too heavily, and while these are necessary in evaluating candidates' experience and qualifications for the job, they do not necessarily speak to the deeper issues of how they will perform according to your company's priorities, and how well they will work within your corporate culture.

Based on the theory that past behavior is the best indicator of future behavior, the "behavioral interview" has become popular in recent years – and with good reason. Behavioral interview questions require the interviewee to provide concrete, narrative examples of past situations. These will often reveal the degree to which s/he possesses the behaviors and traits identified as essential to top performance within your organization. Such questions avoid the typical hypotheticals ("Where do you see yourself in five years?") and instead focus on how an individual has responded to specific situations in the past.

While questions will obviously need to be tailored to the position's responsibilities and context, here are a few examples.

- **Typical Interview Question:** What was your biggest accomplishment in your last job?
  Desired Trait: Creativity
  Revised Question: Describe the most creative work-related project you have carried out, and describe why you succeeded with this project.

- **Typical Interview Question:** Are you a team player?
  Desired Behavior: Collaboration
  Revised Question: Give me an example of a time when you were able to successfully complete a project on a team where there were personality conflicts.

- **Typical Interview Question:** What major challenges and problems did you face at your last job?

  Desired Trait: Resilience

  Revised Question: Describe a difficult situation in which you were able to positively influence others in a desired direction.

Remember to craft questions that are targeted toward the specific behaviors and traits that are unique to your organization. While traits like enthusiasm, patience, selflessness, and optimism may be desired in almost any company, there will be differences in positions' requirements (e.g. travel, a lot of time with clients, management of other staff) that will call for tailored inquiry.

Train all Hiring Managers

Your hiring managers are the first people to encounter most interviewees, and as such they need to be armed not only with a precise understanding of the attributes a candidate needs to succeed, but also with the skills to discover those attributes during an interview. In addition to having the right questions, you need interview staff who can interpret the answers and weight them according to your organization's goals (see Candidate Evaluation Form on page 174).

Training should be mandatory for anyone in your organization responsible for interviewing candidates; Ideally, these training sessions will be underpinned by a clear process and aided by specific tools. Additionally, refresher courses should be offered as the organization's needs evolve.

Training should include the differences between interviewing internal and external candidates for any position. An internal candidate's interview should acknowledge the value of that individual's past contribution to the company, and the knowledge base that s/he possesses. This is important for several reasons. First, it is often smarter (in terms of time and resources) to promote an internal candidate than to hire a new one. Second, the interview process must not disengage existing employees, regardless of whether or not they "win" the promotion. Third, hiring from within is a means to bolster "line of sight" between an individual's career path and the company's goals. And lastly, promotions are an optimal branding and communications opportunity. An internal success story is a powerful reminder of the investment your staff has in your company.

Of course, no firm has a monopoly on all good ideas, approaches, and best practices. Successful companies always complement internal promotions with external hires, thereby ensuring a continuous influx of new ideas.

From the Trenches...

In 1985, while working for the engineering firm Metcalf and Eddy, I was sent off to recruit at MIT. It was an eye-opening experience; my 15 candidates' education and skills were all off the charts. Having been taught to look at these criteria first, I felt a bit stumped regarding whom to invite back for meetings with senior executives. One of my first and best mentors, Ed Burns (Metcalf and Eddy's employment manager at the time), told me "Pick the one person you would love to have over to your house for a cold beer." With that statement, Ed was getting at the essence of the BEST profile years before it crystallized in my head. We had to hire people who were technically brilliant, but who would also interface well with our clients. Of the 15 brilliant individuals I interviewed, Ed's filter was the one I used to narrow things down. They all had the necessary education and skills to perform as an entry level staff engineer. Again, it came down to the behaviors and traits necessary for the job we needed done.

The necessity to hire the best fit for your organization's needs was underscored for me in a conversation I had with a manager from a well-known national nonprofit, during which she reported that the organization's leadership was disengaged because recent budgets hadn't allowed for pay increases or incentive pay. "Well," I reminded her, "You work for a nonprofit. If you're hiring people who want to make a lot of money, you don't yet understand your own engagement drivers." To me, this encounter stands as a prime example of an organization that didn't have an engagement problem – they were simply hiring the wrong people. This underscores the necessity of not only identifying key behaviors and traits, but also of having a comprehensive recruiting strategy.

TOOLS + PROCESSES

BEST Staffing Roadmap

The complex process of interviewing and hiring can be simplified by following a four-step process that begins with needs analysis (identifying the necessary behaviors, education, skills, and traits for a given opening); moves to recruiting and sourcing (which includes resume screening from internal and external candidates); and then expands in the selection process (with interviews, analysis, and the offer). The next step is orientation and integration of the new hire or newly placed internal candidate into the role for which the hire was made, followed by tracking of the employee's development and performance.

To the right is a roadmap, developed with the goal of staffing an organization according to BEST principles, that we implemented at ENSR and have used in LEAP (Leadership Excellence through Advanced Practices) programs and workshops.

BEST STAFFING ROADMAP

Needs Analysis	Recruiting / Resourcing	Selection	Before First Day
Determine Staffing Needs: • Hiring Manager (HM) evaluates long-term strategy and short-term needs BEST Profile: • HM defines success criteria based on BEST profile • HM submits completed profile to HR for approval	Recruiting Strategy: • HM + HR discuss approach to sourcing internal and external candidates • HR posts position to recruiting resources Resume Screening: • HR screens resumes and sends to HM • HM identifies candidates • HM establishes Candidate Evaluation Team to review initial selections	Interview Process: • HM conducts preliminary telephone interview • HM sets up formal interviews • All interviewers prepare to conduct legal, effective interview Top Candidate: • HM selects top candidate + checks references • HM contacts HR to discuss compensation + other details Offer: • HM makes verbal offer; if accepted, HM sends offer letter to candidate Candidate Accepts: • Candidate returns signed letter to HR with start date • HM notifies HR of acceptance	Before First Day: • HR sends HM new hire prep + orientation checklists • HM stays in contact with new hire + continues to "sell" company First Day: • HM initiates orientation with new hire First Week: • Using Employee Development Plan, HM meets with new hire to discuss goals + objectives First Month: • HM meets with employee to plan developmental activities • HM asks retention-related questions Three Months: • HR solicits three-month review + feedback from HM + employee • HM provides three-month feedback; asks retention-related questions; returns signed form to HR.

CANDIDATE EVALUATION FORM

Candidate Being Evaluated: _____

Position: _____

Interviewed By: _____

Date Interviewed: _____

Rating Scale   ### Weighting Factors

Rating Scale	Weighting Factors
3 = Expert / Excellent Match 2 = High / Good Match 1 = Satisfactory / Acceptable 0 = Unsatisfactory	3 = Critical 2 = Important 1 = Helpful

Knowlege / Skills	Rating		Weight		Score
1. Educational Background: What did you like most about your educational experience?		x		=	
2. Technical Skills		x		=	
3. Related Experience		x		=	
Attitude/Habits	**Rating**		**Weight**		**Score**
4. Energy, Drive, Initiative: What are some examples of going beyond your job requirements? Whate are you doing to improve your overall performance?		x		=	
5. Values, Commitment, Goals: How would your work associates describe you? What traits are you most proud of? What best suits you for this job?		x		=	
6. Personality / Cultural Fit: Who was the best manager you ever had? Describe his/her traits. In which prior work environment were you happiest? Why?		x		=	
7. Performance Over Time: How has your job changed since you began working in your field? How would your current manager describe your performance?		x		=	
8. Problem-Solving: What past experience was most stimulating? What kind of problems do you enjoy tackling?		x		=	

Attitude/Habits (Cont.)	Rating		Weight		Score
9. Flexibility / Adaptability: What was the most difficult work adjustment you've had to make?		x		=	
10. Innovation: What approaches would you take to "X" problem (Interviewer to define)?		x		=	
11. Communication: Are you more skilled at written or verbal communication? Why?		x	.	=	
12. Ability to Learn: What kinds of things do you learn quickly? What are most difficult?		x		=	
13. Ability to Learn: What kinds of things do you learn quickly? What are most difficult?		x		=	
14. Client Focus: What past experience best demonstrates your commitment to your / our client?		x		=	
15. Leadership: What are the advantages / disadvantages of working as part of a team? What are the challenges of leading one?		x		=	
16. Ability to Learn: What kinds of things do you learn quickly? What are most difficult?		x		=	
17. Planning / Organization: How do you plan and organize your work? How do you set priorities?		x		=	
18. Relationship Building: How do you build relationships outside your department? Outside the company? How do maintain these relationships over time?		x		=	

Closing Questions + Information:

1. What aspects of the job sound particularly appealing to you?

_____

2. What aspects of the job are of concern to you?

_____

3. References requested? ☐ Yes ☐ No   References to be provided by (date): _____

4. Thank applicant for time commitment.

5. Follow-up time frame given: _____

   Follow-up action: _____

SAMPLE BEHAVIORAL INTERVIEW QUESTIONS

1. Describe a time on any job which you've held in which you were faced with problems or stresses that tested your coping skills. What did you do?

2. Give an example of a time in which you had to be relatively quick in coming to a decision.

3. Can you tell me about a job experience in which you had to speak up in order to be sure that other people knew what you thought or felt?

4. Give me an example of a specific occasion in which you conformed to a policy with which you did not agree.

5. Give me an example of a time in which you had to use your fact-finding skills to gain information for solving a problem. Then, tell me how you analyzed the information to come to a decision.

6. Give me an example of an important goal which you've had and tell me how you reached it.

7. Describe the most significant written document/report/presentation you have had to complete.

8. Give me an example of a time when you had to go above and beyond the call of duty in order to get a job done.

9. Give me an example of a time when you were able to successfully communicate with another person, even though that individual did not like you.

10. Describe a situation in which you were able to effectively "read" another person and guide your actions by your understanding of their individual needs or values.

11. What did you do in your last job in order to be effective? Be specific.

12. Describe the most creative work-related project you have carried out.

13. Describe a time in which you felt it was necessary to modify or change your actions in order to respond to the needs of another person.

14. Give me an example of a time when you had to carefully analyze another person or a situation in order to be effective in your action or decision.

15. What did you do in your last job to contribute to a teamwork environment? Be specific.

16. Give me an example of a problem which you faced on any job you have had, and tell me how you went about solving it.

17. Describe a situation in which you were able to positively influence the actions of others in a desired direction.

Those who initiate change will have a better opportunity to manage the change that is inevitable.

– WILLIAM POLLARD
Physicist

CONCLUSION
SUSTAINING YOUR ENGAGEMENT MODEL

As in any social unit, there is give and take in a corporate culture. Many people in management do not realize the subtle means by which employees will balance an uneven equation by withholding or expanding the traits necessary to make business thrive. Employees will always bring the scale depicted on the following page back into equilibrium. And remember... equilibrium results in discretionary effort.

This is one of the most important lessons of leadership I've learned in my 25 years in business. When I speak to a group of leaders, I will often end my presentation with the simple but powerful visual depicted on the following page.

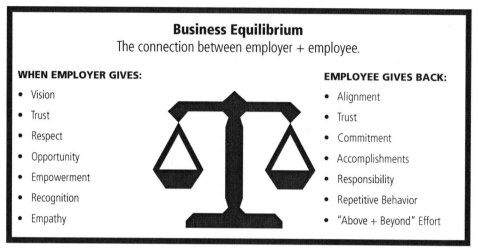

Business Equilibrium
The connection between employer + employee.

WHEN EMPLOYER GIVES:
- Vision
- Trust
- Respect
- Opportunity
- Empowerment
- Recognition
- Empathy

EMPLOYEE GIVES BACK:
- Alignment
- Trust
- Commitment
- Accomplishments
- Responsibility
- Repetitive Behavior
- "Above + Beyond" Effort

Alignment

If a company neglects to articulate a clear vision of the future, it can hardly expect its employees to invest more than the minimum of energy into bringing any future about. Employers or leaders who articulate a clear vision and strategy will learn that employees will help them "get there" quickly and efficiently. Employers or leaders who fail to articulate a clear vision and strategy will soon discover their employees lack alignment with and commitment to their goals. They will be looking at the trees, not the forest – and the goals will be far more difficult to attain.

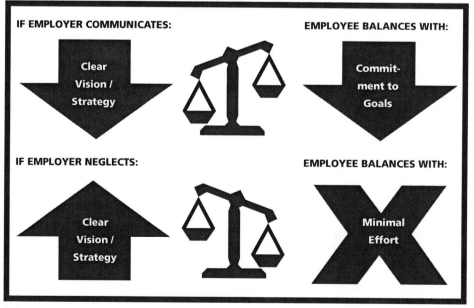

IF EMPLOYER COMMUNICATES:
Clear Vision / Strategy

EMPLOYEE BALANCES WITH:
Commitment to Goals

IF EMPLOYER NEGLECTS:
Clear Vision / Strategy

EMPLOYEE BALANCES WITH:
Minimal Effort

Trust

Trust is the first step toward capturing discretionary effort – the invaluable byproduct of great leadership. If an employer withholds trust, it can hardly expect its employees to trust management in return; but employers who trust their employees will soon see this trust reciprocated.

Paul Spiegelman, CEO of Dallas-based Beryl Corp, hand-writes birthday, get-well, and congratulatory notes to his employees – at times as many as 300 a month! Although turnover in Beryl Corp's industry (managing call centers for the healthcare industry) is historically high, the company exhibits only 1/4th the industry average for turnover while being a leader in profit and growth. In this case, I think the correlation between consideration, respect, and empathy and discretionary effort is quite clear.

Recognition

If exemplary efforts are not recognized, an employer can hardly expect to see more of them. Conversely, a culture of recognition will breed more of the behaviors being commended. (It's worth noting, by the way, that recognition is free!)

Respect

If an employer creates an atmosphere of respect and acknowledges those individuals who go above and beyond, it virtually guarantees greater commitment.

Empathy

The employer or leader who clearly demonstrates care for employees' well being, and exhibits empathy, will see unsurpassed "above and beyond" efforts. Conversely, if employees sense that leadership is indifferent, you can be certain that they will bring the scale back into equilibrium by putting in the bare minimum of effort required to avoid notice. In this scenario, of course, you can forget about discretionary effort.

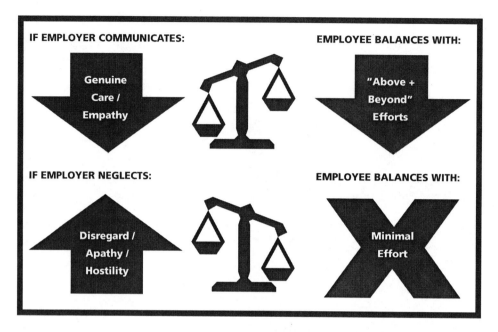

A Final Word

I founded the Employee Engagement Group, and travel the world speaking on the subject, because I have seen firsthand the ways – sometimes overt, sometimes subtle – in which an engaged culture makes for a more robust and sustainable company. Engagement is good for employees; for individual companies; and for the economy at large. While I might stop short of the claim that it's good for society, the benefits that a committed company can deliver within its own community or in larger social realms are quite easy to imagine. So why do so many organizations tend to ignore engagement, or relegate it to the last item on the agenda?

It's natural, and in many ways sensible, for a company to tend to its bottom line first and foremost. Profit is the lifeblood of business, and the obvious link between engagement and profit is not often legible if it is not being measured. The business reasons for engagement (increased discretionary effort, heightened morale, less turnover) do, I think, speak for themselves. But it takes a change in philosophy – not just business practices – to realize those gains.

As a social species, humans' self-interest and our desire for cooperation is a delicate balance that extends to the workplace. This is the very essence of the "business equilibrium" discussed above. And anywhere you look, businesses are, in essence, small societies – with their own priorities, agendas, hierarchies, and norms about which behaviors are:

- Desirable and acceptable, or
- Cause for marginalization or exclusion.

While the primary aim of a company may be to sell X product or service, or make X amount of money, the internal dynamics are not that different than those of a village… or even of a family.

"Engage:" the word shares etymology, and meaning, with *"pledge."*

Make it a pledge. Make good on it. Practice what you preach and remember: your actions speak louder than words.

ENGAGE BOB TO SPEAK AT YOUR FIRM OR CONFERENCE

Bob Kelleher is a sought-after speaker on employee engagement, workforce trends, and leadership. His practical approach and ability to draw on hundreds of best practices, combined with his high-energy delivery, have proven to be a winning formula for conferences, workshops, and keynote presentations across the world.

Call 508/935.8070 to schedule Bob today, or visit *www.BobKelleher.com*.

OTHER SERVICES

Leadership Workshops

Bob's signature 1.5 day leadership workshop, "Engaging Employees To Drive Results," is a must for companies looking to elevate their engagement efforts. If **Louder Than Words** clarifies *what* companies should do, this workshop helps companies and leaders put Bob's practical tools and processes into action (the *how*).

Consulting

Bob is CEO of The Employee Engagement Group, a global leader in helping companies improve their performance through enhanced employee engagement.

Visit *www.EmployeeEngagement.com* for more information.

Drop me a line at rkelleher@ employeeengagement.com to tell me what you thought of this book, share additional best practices, invite me to speak to your leadership team, or simply to say hello. I'd love to hear from you.

To order more books, visit: www.EmployeeEngagement.com.

— *Bob*

Leadership is practiced
not so much in words as in
attitude and in actions.

– HAROLD S. GENEEN
Former CEO, ITT

INDEX